CONTENTS

Introduction

Many feel the kitchen is the heart of the home. This is where families come together, sit and discuss, socialize, and prepare their meals. Often, guests are also entertained in the kitchen. But the kitchen itself has changed dramatically over the years. From décor and styling to appliances, they have evolved from bulky designs, to chic and modern.

Consider how the kitchen appliances have evolved. Modern-day refrigerators first arrived as an icebox in the early 1900s. Over the years, we have seen the coffee maker, blender, juicer, toaster, kettle, dishwasher, stove, microwave, and the pressure cooker.

I am writing this book to introduce you to a new revolution in the kitchen – **The Ninja Foodi Digital Air Fry Oven**.

This magic-appliance promises to deliver much more. It is an 8-in-1 device that does air frying, air roasting, baking, broiling, bagel, toasting, dehydrating, and also helps you keep the food warm. And yet, it is small in size and economical.

With this one device, you will naturally save a lot of space in the kitchen. You don't have to buy 8 separate appliances, so you will save a lot of money as well. There are many other advantages to this product, which I am going to discuss here.

I will also share with you in this book, 80 mouth-watering air fryer recipes that are easy to prepare. I will show you step-by-step how to prepare them.

This book is for everyone who wants to have a smart kitchen, an appliance that saves them cooking time, kitchen space, money, and an appliance that is easy to clean, maintain, and store. I will show you how you can cook quickly with only a few ingredients that are easily available. This will help people who lead a busy lifestyle and are always in limited time.

Thank you for downloading this book. I am sure you will find it very useful.

Happy reading!

Chapter 1 – The Ninja Foodi Digital Air Fry Oven

The Ninja Foodi Digital Air Fry Oven is an awesome new discovery from the Boston, US-based Ninja Kitchen. It is a smart kitchen device that has revolutionized cooking. This 8 in 1 multipurpose gadget offers many cooking functions from one single appliance, so you don't have to buy different things, which naturally will save you a lot of money. It's great for your home because finally, you will have a fully-equipped kitchen that lets you do so many things.

Using the Ninja Foodi Air Fry Oven, you can **Air Fry, Air Roast, Bake, Broil, Bagel, Toast, Dehydrate,** and **Keep Warm**.

It is powerful, customizable as there are many controls, and is very easy to understand and use as well. You will always have complete control over both the cooking temperature and cooking time. This 1800-watt appliance is a powerful device to have in the kitchen as well.

It is very easy to store away this device as well when not in use. All you have to do is just flip it up, which can be done very easily. Thanks to its unique design, the Ninja Foodi Air Fry Oven won't occupy a lot of space on your countertop.

Think of how much space you will save. If you don't have this smart appliance, you would have to buy an air fryer, toaster, and an oven separately, which means so much more money to spend. And that's not all. You will then have to store them separately as well on your kitchen shelf. The Ninja Foodi Air Fry Oven is just a single appliance that can save you all this trouble.

Part A – Features

- Air Fry, Air Roast, Air Broil, Bake, Bagel, Toast, Dehydrate and Keep Warm
- Air fry 4 pounds fried food, 75% less fat than traditional methods of frying
- Cooks 60% faster compared to a traditional oven
- 60 second preheat
- Cooks full meals in only 20 minutes
- 40% more even baking than other appliances
- 45% larger pan cooking area compared to flat surface areas of others
- Dial selector
- Programmable
- Warm and preheat functions
- Versatile airflow system
- Fits a 13-inch pizza, 9 toast slices, 6 chicken breasts
- Toast darkness selector
- Cancel button
- Auto shut off

- 1800 watts
- Stay-cool handles
- Easy cleaning, removable crumb tray
- Dishwasher safe
- Digital Crisp Control technology
- 1-year limited manufacturer warranty
- Instruction guide

Includes:
- Chrome-plated wire rack
- 13 x 13-inch air fry basket, dishwasher safe
- 13 x 13-inch sheet pan, dishwasher safe
- Removable crumb tray
- 1750-watt oven

Part B – Structural Composition

On unboxing this Ninja product, you will see a rectangular appliance that has a
- Width of 19.7 inches
- Height of 7.5 inches
- Depth of 15.1 inches

You will also see a control panel at the front side and a flip lid. On the inside, there are side panels where the steel rack is inserted and the sheet pan is placed. Its sheet pan, crumb tray, and air fryer basket can all be removed. They are also dishwasher safe.

The crumb tray of the unit is inside. Food droppings won't fall into the oven base thanks to its position at the bottom of the oven. Insert this tray every time you are cooking. Use the sheet pan for broiling, toasting, or baking. On the other hand, the air fryer basket is to fry the food evenly. You can also use the air rack for roasting.

Part C – The Control Panel

There is an LED screen on the top of the control panel. It displays time in minutes and hours. Temperature is also displayed in Fahrenheit. You will see 'Pre' on the LED screen in red if the appliance is preheating or 'Hot' if you have to give it a break for cooling. The LED will turn to 'Flip' once it has cooled down enough. This sign means that it can be flipped for vertical storage.

There are icons that also show whether the device is set to Celsius or Fahrenheit. The function you select is lit up when you turn the oven on. Inside the oven, you will find a light bulb that will help you find out whether the food is done while it is being cooked inside the Ninja.

The oven's functions and modes are below the LED panel. This multifunctional dial both starts and pauses the oven. There are 'Temp' and 'Time' buttons for adjusting the temperature and time. You will be able to adjust the darkness level and the number of slices while toasting too. Rotate this dial to easily change from one mode to another. There will be a blue light beside the mode you have selected.

Its power key is for obvious purpose – to switch the appliance 'On' and 'Off'. These buttons are located close to the control panel's bottom.

The Bagel and Toast modes don't display the temperature and time. They show the darkness level and the number of slices.

Part D – Instruction Guide

This Ninja Kitchen oven comes with an instruction guide, which is extremely detailed and easy to understand. It covers virtually everything you need to know. This will help you understand its functions, settings, and use. The guide will also help you clean the gadget and store it away when not in use.

Part E – Warranty

The Ninja® Foodi™ Digital Air Fry Oven comes with a 1-year limited warranty from the manufacturer, Ninja Kitchen. There is also a 60-day money-back guarantee in the unlikely event that you are unhappy with this product.

Chapter 2 - Ninja Foodi Digital Air Fry Oven Benefits

The Ninja® Foodi™ Digital Air Fry Oven has quickly become a top-selling kitchen appliance because of its many benefits. Here are its top benefits –

1.   A multi-purpose device – This is an 8 in 1 device that lets you use it for several functions. As I have mentioned already, you can use this appliance for air frying, air roasting, baking, toasting bread, bagel, to broil food and dehydrate. And you can do all that with just the press of a button. While using the Ninja, you will also be able to switch from one mode to another while cooking. In the bagel and toast function, you can decide the bread darkness you want.

2.   Flip-up for storing – It has an adjustable flip function unlike most other conventional air fryers of ovens you will find. Because of this, you will be able to keep the oven both vertically and horizontally on your kitchen shelf. When cooking, it should be in a horizontal position. But when you are not using it, just clean the oven, and flip it up. It will stand vertically on your shelf. This will give you more space on the shelf. Make sure that the device is properly cleaned. In fact, it takes 50% less space on the kitchen shelf flipped up.

3.   No more toasters – In your Ninja® Foodi™ Digital Air Fry Oven, you will also find a very useful toaster. This will give you 2 options for toasting bread and bagel. Just press the toast button for bread. You will also find the bagel mode, which you must use for toasting bagel. Press the 'Darkness' and the 'Slices' buttons to adjust temperature and time. With this function, you can have both crispy dark brown and soft light brown toasts as you desire.

4.   Even and fast cooking – The unique design of this appliance promotes speed and provides an even cooking result. Its 60 seconds preheat and quick family-sized meal cooking features are very handy. It does up to 40% more even baking compared to similar products. The pan cooking area is 45% larger in this device compared to appliances with a flat surface area. So the Ninja can accommodate up to 6 chicken breasts of 6 to 8 oz. each, 9 toast slices, and a 13-inch pizza.

5.   Healthier – 75% less fat compared to traditional frying methods in the air frying function. This has been tested and confirmed for hand-cut and deep-fried French fries.

6.   Time, energy-efficient – Ninja Kitchen is widely regarded for making energy-efficient products. The technology used in this appliance is advanced. Working at 1750 watts an hour, it preheats fast to attain the desired temperature. This appliance can bake warm and air fry quickly, which saves you energy and time. The Ninja® Foodi™ Digital Air Fry Oven can cook 60% faster compared to a traditional oven that has air roast.

7.   It can be cleaned easily – Cleaning and maintenance are easy. The crumb tray is removable. You will also be able to access the back panel easily for times when you want to deep clean.

8.   User-friendly – All features including the control panel is extremely user-friendly. Push-button technology. All the buttons are clearly marked for easy understanding. Each function has a different button. There are dials for switching from one mode to another and to decrease or increase the temperature and cooking time. Press these same dials for pausing or starting a function.

9.   High technology – This Ninja appliance is a high-tech gadget. Thanks to the use of Digital Crisp Control Technology, it has precise fan speeds and controlled temperatures that deliver very good results for all the functions. This ensures you have a really versatile appliance in your kitchen.

Pros

- Offers great value because of its many functions
- Preheats very quickly in just 60 seconds
- Cooks evenly
- Works very quietly
- A very good control panel that can be understood and operated with ease
- Easy to store as it can be flipped easily
- Will occupy less space on your countertop
- Easy to clean
- Extremely versatile gadget

Cons

- Can be costly for some buyers
- The manufacturer warranty could be longer

Chapter 3 – Operation, Functions and Tips

The Ninja Foodi Digital Air Fry Oven is extremely easy to use and offers as many as 8 great functions, making it a top choice for the kitchen. You will have complete control over the cooking process with just 1 dial.

First, select the cooking function (air fry, air roast, air broil, bake, toast, bagel, dehydrate, keep warm) by using the dial. After doing this, set the temperature (or the toasting level) and time. The cooking process is now ready to start. Just press the dial. You can also pause cooking with the timer, which is very useful when you have to add ingredients or stir.

The Ninja oven can switch easily between Celsius and Fahrenheit. The control panel also tells you when the appliance is preheating and when it has become cool enough for cleaning or flipping to store. You should be able to read the temperature display (or the darkness level for bagels and toast, and the number of slices) and the timer easily. The temperature and time both are default to your last used settings.

Settings and Functions

There are 8 settings in this versatile gadget, which I am sure will help you immensely.

• Air Frying – A good choice when you have to deep fry to get a crisp exterior. It can air fry 4 pounds of food at once. To do this, first, go to this setting. The appliance will use high heat and maximum convection speed from both the bottom and top elements. You can set the time to 1 hour. You can also adjust the temperature between 250 and 450 degrees F.

• Air Roasting – The oven is used for air roasting. Use this setting while cooking different types of sheet pan recipes. This setting will use medium convection fan speed. The heat will be even from both the bottom and top elements. You can adjust both the temperature and time as well. Set the time to 2 hours and the temperature between 250 and 450 degrees F. All the ingredients will come out light brown and tender.

• Air Broiling – This is somewhat different. The setting will use the high heat from the top element and medium convection fan speed to deliver well-cooked food and good searing you expect from broiling. Set the time to 30 minutes. You can choose to set the temperature to either Low or High. This is a good setting for browning fish or chicken fillets, steaks, or chops.

• Baking – Unlike the settings, I have mentioned above, here no fan is used. The heat from the bottom and top elements aren't used as well. You won't be able to bake an entire loaf here. However, it does bake muffins or cakes in its shallow pan very well. You can also bake small items, such as cookies on its sheet pan. Baking biscuit is a lot of fun in this setting. You should also be able to warm pita bread for sandwiches or tortillas for tacos.

- This is good for dishes that are delicate in nature. Set the time to 2 hours, and adjust the temperature between 250 and 450 degrees F.
- Toasting – The Ninja® Foodi™ Digital Air Fry Oven's toast setting doesn't use a fan or heat from the bottom and top elements. It can accommodate and toast up to 9 bread slices at once without squishing them. The toasting and browning are done evenly. The golden brown shade is such a pleasure to see. How long it takes to achieve the result is decided automatically by the device, depending on the number of bread slices you are toasting. You don't have to adjust the temperature. All you have to do is just decide whether you want to get your toast done lightly or dark. So you don't have to stay pinned beside the machine, checking whether your toasting is correct or not. It won't burn ever.
- Bagel – This setting too doesn't use a fan. The heat is from the top and it is slightly lower. It can toast up to 6 slices of bagels at one time. And like the toasting function, here too, you won't find any temperature adjustment. The time needed is also decided automatically, depending on how many slices of bagels you are toasting.
- Dehydrating – It has a wide airy dry basket that can accommodate more food than most other air fryers. The Ninja can also dry decent food amounts. This machine will work quietly as well.
- Keep Warm – Try this setting and I am sure that you will be pleased with the result. You may be able to keep the food warm at serving temperature for up to 2 hours, but remember, many foods can get too dried out if you leave it for that long. You can use this function or just your microwave to reheat the food. If you don't have a microwave, then this Ninja will do the job for you well.

Cleaning and Maintenance

Cleaning this appliance is super-easy as you will find I am sure. The entire meal is prepared on a pan, which makes cleaning an easy job. Its sheet pan is dishwasher safe and nonstick. Crumb tray of the Ninja protects the oven's bottom against spills. It slides out easily so that you can wash. You will be able to clean the oven as well. The oven's back opens completely, which allows you to clean the entire surface properly. Just use dish soap and warm water for this. Wipe clean the outside using a sponge. You can then flip up the unit for storage.

- Remember to give your Ninja time to cool down after every use. Do not start to clean before it. The 'Red' sign will tell you that it is cooling.
- You will see the 'Flip' sign on the screen once it has cooled down. The 'Hot' sign will disappear. It is now ready for cleaning.
- Unplug your air fry open now carefully so that the power supply is cut off.
- You are now ready to take out all the removable parts from the oven's inside, which includes the wire rack, sheet pan, crumb tray, and the air fryer basket. Use soapy water or dishwasher to wash them properly. Allow them to dry before using again.

- Hold its handle under the lid. Now push the front up to flip your oven.
- Pull the oven's base. Like the lid this too will come out.
- Take a wet cloth and wipe the base.
- Give it time so that the base has become dry completely before closing it.
- Your Ninja Foodi Digital Air Fry Oven is ready to be used again.

Safety Tips

Here are some important tips to help you use the appliance safely.

Do not overload	This is a powerful gadget, but the air fryer is still a small oven. You would surely not stack your chicken breasts on top of each other in a regular oven. This is true with the Ninja as well. Spread them out so that the basket isn't overloaded. Air cannot circulate well if you include too many things into the air fryer basket. The food will not be that crispy. So cook in batches if you have to prepare a lot of anything. Remember this, especially with diced veggies, fries, and small items that you want to be crispy.
Don't forget to pre-heat	Give it the time for preheating. It only takes 60 seconds anyway. The air fryer should be set to proper temperature before you start the cooking, because that is when you will get optimum cooking. The air flow and temperature will be at the right level, which will ensure that the cooked food will be crispy and perfect. You may not get good results if you just toss the food into the oven.
Cleaning	Don't make the mistake of washing incorrectly or infrequently. It is a good idea to hand wash after every use. Almost every recipe you prepare will have some crumbs or debris left behind. The food particles that remain may burn quickly when you fire up the gadget the next time. This may cause both smell and smoke. It may also ruin the food you are cooking. Cleaning this Ninja is very easy as the parts are removable. Just use some warm water or dishwasher. Follow the process I have described above. You can also use a nonstick spray, but make sure that it is not an aerosol cooking spray, as they may damage the air fryer. Always clean properly before you add food.
Parchment paper/foil	There are some messy foods, such as wings that are coated in sticky sauce. It is always better to have them on a sheet of parchment or tinfoil paper in the basket of your air fryer. This will make clean up so much easier. But make sure that the food is heavy so that it is weighed down. Otherwise, the sheets may fly around because of the circulating hot air.
Space in	Air fryers work by circulating hot air to make the food crisp. This

the air fry is why you must have enough space around it so that the air can flow easily. The best practice is to keep about 5 inches of space on all sides. It is never a good idea if your appliance is pushed against the wall.

FAQs about Ninja Foodi Air Fry Oven

Q). What Are the different functions for?

A). Your Ninja® Foodi™ Digital Air Fry Oven has 8 functions.

<u>Air Fry</u> – For making fried foods like French fries, chicken wings, and chicken nuggets with very little or no oil.

<u>Air Roast</u> – To get very well cooked inside but a crispy outside like roasted veggies and pan meals.

<u>Air Broil</u> – To broil fish and meat evenly.

<u>Bake</u> – For baking homemade pizza and cookies.

<u>Bagel</u> – You can toast up to 9 bagels on its wire rack.

<u>Toast</u> – Toast up to 9 bread slices evenly and achieve the right desired darkness.

<u>Dehydrate</u> – To dehydrate vegetables, fruits, meats, and healthy snacks.

<u>Keep Warm</u> – This function keeps your food warm.

Q). What is each function's temperature range?

A). <u>Air Fry</u> – 250°F to 450°F, <u>Air Roast</u> – 250°F to 450°F, <u>Air Broil</u> – 350°F for low and 450°F for high, <u>Bake</u> – 250°F to 400°F, <u>Toast</u> – 450°F, <u>Dehydrate</u> – 105°F to 195°F, <u>Keep Warm</u> – 165°F

Q). Is its fry basket non-stick?

A). No. Apply cooking spray to make the sticking minimum.

Q). What is the capacity of its air fry basket?

A). It can hold 4 pounds of food maximum.

Q). Can I bake a 13 x 9-inch cake?

A). Yes, you can do this in the oven. It will accommodate a cake of this size.

Q). Can I use a 9 x 13-inch pan in this oven?

A). Yes, you can do so.

Q). Why does the fan continue to run even though the unit is off?

A). Yes, it will run even after the cooking is done. This is important to cool the unit's internal components so that you can flip your Ninja quickly.

Q). Why does the fan run when you work the air fry and bake functions?

A). The control fan will turn on automatically during these functions. This keeps the panel cook during cooking.

Q). Can I remove the front glass door?

A). No. You cannot remove the door.

Q). What is the Ninja's exterior made of?

A). It is made of stainless steel.

Q). Will the oven's exterior become hot?

A). Its glass window and exterior portion will become hot while you are cooking. However, the door handle and its control panel will stay cool, so you can touch.

Q). How should I store the air fry oven?

A). It is easy. Just hold the handles you will find on both sides of the oven. Lift and flip on its side. Then keep it upright position while deep cleaning or storing.

Q). Do I need to do something special while folding the oven up when storing?

A). Just remember to keep your unit 5 inches away from the wall. Give it time to cool down. If the oven is On, the Flip will be displayed when it has become cool enough. You don't have to push any buttons or levers to fold it up. There is nothing to be done to lock it in place as well. It will not fall. The air fry basket and rack will be in place as you fold up the unit. The sheet pan too will be in place.

Q). Can I keep the sheet pan and the air fry basket on the countertop?

A). Make sure that you keep them only on heat-safe surfaces. Be careful as they will become hot while cooking.

Q). Can I use any other cookware not provided by Ninja?

A). Yes, you can other sheet pans. But remember, the usual half sheet pan won't fit. You can go for a quarter sheet pan or something smaller. Ninja sheet pans optimizes the surface area as it has been made especially for this digital fry oven. A muffin tin for 6 cups and a 13-inch baking pan will also fit. You can use ovenproof ceramic baking dishes, but make sure that they aren't too deep. Avoid anything that is not broiler safe.

Chapter 4 – 21-Day Good Health Food Plan

Some of us are rich, while others could do with some more money. No matter what you are, always remember, **health is the real wealth we have**. You may have a world of riches, but what is the point of it, if you don't have the health to enjoy the money.

The good news is you can easily improve your health considerably by choosing to eat the right foods. It may take only 21 days to start your journey towards a healthier way of living.

The plan is designed to help you improve health and even reduce weight by eating the right foods, cooking it the right way, through portion control, and doing exercises daily. You will have to eat a balanced meal that includes proteins, carbs, lots of fresh fruits and vegetables, and healthy fats. Take your meals at the right times, in the correct portions, eat from different food groups so you have plenty of options, and reduce the intake of unhealthy foods. You will see a positive change in just 3 weeks.

It is important to remember that you must never skip your meals. Have a quick breakfast in the morning before leaving for work. If you are always rushing to work in the morning, then plan to prepare something the night before. Also, sit down to have your meals. A meal on the go is not a good idea.

Food Timings

1.   Breakfast at 9 AM
2.   Lunch at 1 PM
3.   Dinner at 6 PM
4.   Snacks at 11 AM, 3 PM, and 8 PM

21-Day Healthy Food Recipes

Here are some food ideas that I am sure will give you better health in 21 days.

Breakfast Recipes

1.   **Baked Oatmeal with Bananas and Berries**

Made with – Eggs, bananas, honey, rolled oats, ground cinnamon, baking powder, almond milk, and blueberries.
Prep Time: 15 minutes, **Cook Time:** 30 minutes, **Servings**: 12
Nutrition Info Per Serving: Calories: 112, Fat: 2 g, Carbohydrates: 20 g, Sugar: 5 g, Protein: 4 g, Cholesterol: 31 mg, Fiber: 3 g

2.   **Zucchini Noodle Bowl**

Made with – Sweet potatoes, olive oil, ripe avocado, chopped garlic, zucchini, water, lemon juice, eggs, sea salt, and chopped green onions.
Prep Time: 15 minutes, **Cook Time:** 43 minutes, **Servings**: 2
Nutrition Info Per Serving: Calories: 342, Fat: 18 g, Carbohydrates: 37 g, Sugar: 13 g, Protein: 13 g, Cholesterol: 183 mg, Fiber: 10 g

3. **Pumpkin Pancakes**

Made with – Pumpkin puree, almond milk, egg whites, vanilla extract, oats, whey protein powder, ground cinnamon and nutmeg, baking powder, and Greek yogurt.

Prep Time: 15 minutes, **Cook Time:** 20 minutes, **Servings**: 2

Nutrition Info Per Serving: Calories: 317, Fat: 1 g, Carbohydrates: 47 g, Sugar: 9 g, Protein: 22 g, Cholesterol: 8 mg, Fiber: 12 g

Lunch Recipes

1. **Avocado and Shrimp Lettuce Wraps**

Made with – Shredded cole slaw mix, lime juice, honey, chopped cilantro, shrimp (deveined, peeled), cumin, chili powder, garlic powder, cayenne powder, paprika, salt, and olive oil.

Prep Time: 15 minutes, **Cook Time:** 20 minutes, **Servings**: 1

Nutrition Info Per Serving: Calories: 256, Fat: 18 g, Carbohydrates: 16 g, Sugar: 4 g, Protein: 14 g, Cholesterol: 116 mg, Fiber: 10 g

2. **Pasta Salad**

Made with – Veggie macaroni, baby spinach, red pepper, sliced olives, marinated tomatoes, crumbled feta cheese, and pesto vinaigrette.

Prep Time: 2 hours, **Cook Time:** 10 minutes, **Servings**: 8

Nutrition Info Per Serving: Calories: 464, Fat: 25 g, Carbohydrates: 51 g, Sugar: 7 g, Protein: 10 g, Cholesterol: 8 mg, Fiber: 7 g

3. **Turkey Burgers**

Made with – Ground turkey, chili powder, cumin, onion and garlic powder, salt, avocados, lime juice, garlic powder, and olive oil.

Prep Time: 10 minutes, **Cook Time:** 20 minutes, **Servings**: 3

Nutrition Info Per Serving: Calories: 316, Fat: 21 g, Carbohydrates: 9 g, Sugar: 0 g, Protein: 24 g, Cholesterol: 80 mg, Fiber: 8 g

Dinner Recipes

1. **Crispy Chicken Parmesan**

Made with – Skinless and boneless chicken breast strips, mayo, parmesan cheese, paprika, pepper, and salt.

Prep Time: 15 minutes, **Cook Time:** 30 minutes, **Servings**: 4

Nutrition Info Per Serving: Calories: 274, Fat: 14 g, Carbohydrates: 1 g, Sugar: 4 g, Protein: 33 g, Cholesterol: 92 mg

2. **Chicken Slow Cooker Soup**

Made with – Chicken breast, olive oil, diced onion, chopped and peeled onion, celery, minced garlic, brown rice flour, chicken stock, Greek yogurt, peas, corn, jicama, pepper, and Italian seasoning.

Prep Time: 15 minutes, **Cook Time:** 5-6 hours, **Servings**: 6

Nutrition Info Per Serving: Calories: 250, Fat: 5 g, Carbohydrates: 28 g, Sugar: 7 g,

Protein: 26 g, Cholesterol: 50 mg, Fiber: 6 g

3.   Crab Cakes with Sweet Potato

Made with – Cooked crab, mashed and cooked sweet potato, red bell pepper, green onion, egg, garlic, chopped parsley, lemon juice, creole seasoning, pepper, bread crumbs, coconut oil.

Prep Time: 10 minutes, **Cook Time:** 15 minutes, **Servings:** 6

Nutrition Info Per Serving: Calories: 218, Fat: 9 g, Carbohydrates: 17 g, Sugar: 3 g, Protein: 15 g, Cholesterol: 84 mg, Fiber: 2 g

Dessert Recipes

1.   Blueberry Pudding

Made with – Eggs, almond milk, maple syrup, vanilla extract, nutmeg, sea salt, cubed whole grain bread, blueberries, cooking spray, hot water.

Prep Time: 15 minutes, **Cook Time:** 1 hour, 20 minutes, **Servings:** 8

Nutrition Info Per Serving: Calories: 235, Fat: 7 g, Carbohydrates: 33 g, Sugar: 14 g, Protein: 11 g, Cholesterol: 186 mg, Fiber: 5 g

2.   Chocolate Peanut Butter Pie

Made with – Low fat milk, tofu, chocolate scoops, peanut butter, banana, raw honey, whole wheat pie crust.

Prep Time: 10 minutes, **Cook Time:** 1 hour, **Servings:** 12

Nutrition Info Per Serving: Calories: 248, Fat: 14 g, Carbohydrates: 20 g, Sugar: 9 g, Protein: 13 g, Cholesterol: 2 mg, Fiber: 3 g

Exercise Daily

Let me say this once more – only food cannot help you attain better health. It is absolutely essential that you also do daily exercises. If that seems too much, then you must at least workout for 5 days a week.

Far too many of us are leading a sedentary lifestyle these days, and this is impacting our health negatively. We are going to work in our cars, taking the elevator up to our offices, and enjoying the conveniences and comforts of modern living. Many of us are not even walking 100 meters a day.

Change all that.

* Join a health club and get some exercise.
* Do some cardio exercises, but focus on your entire body.
* You can also join a yoga class.
* Some aerobic programs on TV are very good. You can follow them too.

There are alternatives if you cannot do workouts for some reason. For instance, you can do jogging or running in the morning, or at least some brisk walking. But make sure that you are sweating while walking/

You can also do cycling, swimming, or take up a sport, such as tennis, squash, or basketball. A competitive game will give you a good workout.

Chapter 5 – Air Fryer Oven Recipes

Here are some very good air fry oven recipes for breakfast, snacks, desserts, lunch, and dinner. Check them out. Prepare as many as you like.

Breakfast and Brunch

Banana Bread

Prep Time: 15 minutes, Cook Time: 45 minutes, Serves: 8

Ingredients:
- ¾ cup whole wheat flour
- 2 medium ripe mashed bananas
- 2 large eggs
- 1 teaspoon of Vanilla extract
- ¼ teaspoon Baking soda
- ½ cup granulated sugar

Instructions:
1. Keep parchment paper at the bottom of your pan. Apply some cooking spray.
2. Whisk together the baking soda, salt, flour, and cinnamon (optional) in a bowl.
3. Keep it aside.
4. Take another bowl and bring together the eggs, bananas, vanilla, and yogurt (optional) in it.
5. Stir the wet ingredients gently into your flour mix. Combine well.
6. Now pour your batter into the pan. You can also sprinkle some walnuts.
7. Heat your air fryer to 310°F. Cook till it turns brown.
8. Keep the bread on your wire rack so that it cools in the pan. Slice.

Nutrition Facts Per Serving

Calories 240, Carbohydrates 29g, Total Fat 12g, Protein 4g, Fiber 2g, Sodium 184mg, Sugars 17g

Sweet Potato Tots

Prep Time: 20 minutes, Cook Time: 1 hour, Serves: 4

Ingredients:

- 1 tablespoon of potato starch
- 2 small sweet potatoes, peeled
- 1-1/4 teaspoons kosher salt
- 1/8 teaspoon of garlic powder
- ¾ cup ketchup

Instructions:

1. Boil water in a medium-sized pot over high heat.
2. Add the potatoes. Cook till it becomes tender. Transfer them to a plate for cooling. Grate them in a mid-sized bowl.
3. Toss gently with garlic powder, 1 teaspoon of salt, and potato starch.
4. Shape the mix into tot-shaped cylinders.
5. Apply cooking spray on the air fryer basket.
6. Place half of the tots in a later in your basket. Apply some cooking spray.
7. Cook till it becomes light brown at 400°F.
8. Take out from the frying basket. Sprinkle some salt.
9. Serve with ketchup immediately.

Nutrition Facts Per Serving

Calories 80, Carbohydrates 19g, Total Fat 0g, Protein 1g, Fiber 2g, Sodium 335mg, Sugars 8g

Breakfast Frittata

Prep Time: 15 minutes, Cook Time: 20 minutes, Serves: 2

Ingredients:

- 4 eggs, beaten lightly
- 4 oz. sausages, cooked and crumbled
- 1 onion, chopped
- 2 tablespoons of red bell pepper, diced
- ½ cup shredded Cheddar cheese

Instructions:

1. Bring together the cheese, eggs, sausage, onion, and bell pepper in a bowl.
2. Mix well.
3. Preheat your air fryer to 180 degrees C or 360 degrees F.
4. Apply cooking spray lightly.
5. Keep your egg mix in a prepared cake pan.
6. Now cook in your air fryer till the frittata has become set.

Nutrition Facts Per Serving

Calories 487, Carbohydrates 3g, Cholesterol 443mg, Total Fat 39g, Protein 31g, Fiber 0.4g, Sodium 694mg, Sugars 1g

Loaded Potatoes

Prep Time: 10 minutes, Cook Time: 15 minutes, Serves: 2

Ingredients:

- 11 oz. baby potatoes
- 2 cut bacon slices
- 1-1/2 oz. low-fat cheddar cheese, shredded
- 1 teaspoon of olive oil
- 2 tablespoons low-fat sour cream

Instructions:

1. Toss the potatoes with oil.
2. Place them in your air fryer basket. Cook till they get tender at 350°F. stir occasionally.
3. Cook the bacon meanwhile in a skillet till it gets crispy.
4. Take out the bacon from your pan. Crumble.
5. Keep the potatoes on a serving plate. Crush them lightly to split.
6. Top with cheese, chives, salt, crumbled bacon, and sour cream.

Nutrition Facts Per Serving

Calories 240, Carbohydrates 26g, Total Fat 12g, Protein 7g, Fiber 4g, Sodium 287mg, Sugars 3g

Cinnamon and Sugar Doughnuts

Prep Time: 25 minutes, Cook Time: 16 minutes, Serves: 9

Ingredients:
- 1 teaspoon cinnamon
- 1/3 cup of white sugar
- 2 large egg yolks
- 2-1/2 tablespoons of butter, room temperature
- 1-1/2 teaspoons baking powder
- 2-1/4 cups of all-purpose flour

Instructions:
1. Take a bowl and press your butter and white sugar together in it.
2. Add the egg yolks. Stir till it combines well.
3. Now sift the baking powder, flour, and salt in another bowl.
4. Keep one-third of the flour mix and half of the sour cream into your egg-sugar mixture. Stir till it combines well.
5. Now mix the remaining sour cream and flour. Refrigerate till you can use it.
6. Bring together the cinnamon and one-third sugar in your bowl.
7. Roll half-inch-thick dough.
8. Cut large slices (9) in this dough. Create a small circle in the center. This will make doughnut shapes.
9. Preheat your fryer to 175 degrees C or 350 degrees F.
10. Brush melted butter on both sides of your doughnut.
11. Keep half of the doughnuts in the air fryer's basket.
12. Apply the remaining butter on the cooked doughnuts.
13. Dip into the sugar-cinnamon mix immediately.

Nutrition Facts Per Serving

Calories 336, Carbohydrates 44g, Cholesterol 66mg, Total Fat 16g, Protein 4g, Fiber 1g, Sodium 390mg, Sugars 19g

Tex-Mex Hash Browns

Prep Time: 15 minutes, Cook Time: 30 minutes, Serves: 4

Ingredients:

- 1-1/2 24 oz. potatoes, cut and peeled
- 1 onion, cut into small pieces
- 1 tablespoon of olive oil
- 1 jalapeno, seeded and cut
- 1 red bell pepper, seeded and cut

Instructions:

1. Soak the potatoes in water.
2. Preheat your air fryer to 160 degrees C or 320 degrees F.
3. Drain and dry the potatoes using a clean towel.
4. Keep in a bowl.
5. Drizzle some olive oil over the potatoes, coat well.
6. Transfer to the air frying basket.
7. Add the onion, jalapeno, and bell pepper in the bowl.
8. Sprinkle half teaspoon olive oil, pepper, and salt. Coat well by tossing.
9. Now transfer your potatoes to the bowl with the veg mix from your fryer.
10. Place the empty basket into the air fryer. Raise the temperature to 180 degrees C or 356 degrees F.
11. Toss the contents of your bowl for mixing the potatoes with the vegetables evenly.
12. Transfer mix into the basket.
13. Cook until the potatoes have become crispy and brown.

Nutrition Facts Per Serving

Calories 197, Carbohydrates 34g, Cholesterol 0mg, Total Fat 5g, Protein 4g, Fiber 5g, Sodium 79mg, Sugars 3g

French Toast Sticks

Prep Time: 10 minutes, Cook Time: 10 minutes, Serves: 2

Ingredients:

- 4 slices of thick bread
- 2 eggs, lightly beaten
- 1 teaspoon cinnamon
- 1 teaspoon of vanilla extract
- ¼ cup milk

Instructions:

1. Cut the bread into slices for making sticks.
2. Keep parchment paper on the air fryer basket's bottom.
3. Preheat your air fryer to 180 degrees C or 360 degrees F.
4. Now stir together the milk, eggs, cinnamon, vanilla extract, and nutmeg (optional). Combine well.
5. Dip each bread piece into the egg mix. Submerge well.
6. Remove the excess fluid by shaking it well.
7. Keep them in the fryer basket in a single layer.
8. Cook without overcrowding your fryer.

Nutrition Facts Per Serving

Calories 241, Carbohydrates 29g, Cholesterol 188mg, Total Fat 9g, Protein 11g, Fiber 2g, Sodium 423mg, Sugars 4g

Sausage Patties

Prep Time: 5 minutes, Cook Time: 10 minutes, Serves: 4

Ingredients:

- 1 pack sausage patties
- 1 serving cooking spray

Instructions:

1. Preheat your air fryer to 200 degrees C or 400 degrees F.
2. Keep the sausage patties in a basket. Work in batches if needed.
3. Cook for 3 minutes.
4. Turn the sausage over and cook for another 2 minutes.

Nutrition Facts Per Serving

Calories 168, Carbohydrates 1g, Cholesterol 46mg, Total Fat 12g, Protein 14g, Fiber 0g, Sodium 393mg, Sugars 1g

Roasted Cauliflower

Prep Time: 10 minutes, Cook Time: 15 minutes, Serves: 2

Ingredients:

- 4 cups of cauliflower florets
- 1 tablespoon peanut oil
- 3 cloves garlic
- ½ teaspoon smoked paprika
- ½ teaspoon of salt

Instructions:

1. Preheat your air fryer to 200 degrees C or 400 degrees F.
2. Now cut the garlic into half. Use a knife to smash it.
3. Keep in a bowl with salt, paprika, and oil.
4. Add the cauliflower. Coat well.
5. Transfer the coated cauliflower to your air fryer.
6. Cook for 10 minutes. Shake after 5 minutes.

Nutrition Facts Per Serving

Calories 136, Carbohydrates 12g, Cholesterol 0mg, Total Fat 8g, Protein 4g, Fiber 5.3g, Sodium 642mg, Sugars 5g

Garlic Cheese Bread

Prep Time: 5 minutes, Cook Time: 10 minutes, Serves: 2

Ingredients:

- 1 cup mozzarella cheese, shredded
- 1 large egg
- ¼ cup parmesan cheese, grated
- ½ teaspoon garlic powder

Instructions:

1. Use parchment paper to line your air fryer basket.
2. Bring together the parmesan cheese, mozzarella cheese, garlic powder, and egg in your bowl.
3. Mix until it combines well.
4. Now create a round circle on the parchment paper in your fryer basket.
5. Heat your air fryer to 175 degrees C or 350 degrees F.
6. Fry the bread. Take out and serve warm.

Nutrition Facts Per Serving

Calories 294, Carbohydrates 3g, Cholesterol 138mg, Total Fat 22g, Protein 21g, Fiber 0.1g, Sodium 538mg, Sugars 1g

Fish and Seafood

Crumbed Fish

Prep Time: 10 minutes, Cook Time: 12 minutes, Serves: 4

Ingredients:

- 4 flounder fillets
- 1 cup bread crumbs
- 1 egg, beaten
- ¼ cup of vegetable oil
- 1 lemon, sliced

Instructions:

1. Preheat your air fryer to 180 degrees C or 350 degrees F.
2. Mix the oil and bread crumbs in a bowl. Keep stirring until you see this mixture becoming crumbly and loose.
3. Now dip your fish fillets into the egg. Remove any excess.
4. Dip your fillets into the bread crumb mix. Make sure to coat evenly.
5. Keep the coated fillets in your preheated fryer gently.
6. Cook until you see the fish flaking easily with a fork.
7. Add lemon slices for garnishing.

Nutrition Facts Per Serving

Calories 389, Carbohydrates 23g, Cholesterol 107mg, Total Fat 21g, Protein 27g, Fiber 3g, Sodium 309mg, Sugars 2g

Zesty Fish Fillets

Prep Time: 5 minutes, Cook Time: 12 minutes, Serves: 4

Ingredients:
- 4 fillets of salmon or tilapia
- 2-1/2 teaspoons vegetable oil
- ¾ cups crushed cornflakes or bread crumbs
- 2 eggs, beaten
- 1 packet dry dressing mix

Instructions:
1. Preheat the air fryer to 180° C.
2. Mix the dressing mix and the breadcrumbs together.
3. Pour the oil. Stir until you see the mix getting crumbly and loose.
4. Now dip your fish fillets into the egg. Remove the excess.
5. Dip your fillets into the crumb mix. Coat evenly.
6. Transfer to the fryer carefully.
7. Cook for 10 minutes. Take out and serve.
8. You can also add some lemon wedges on your fish.

Nutrition Facts Per Serving

Calories 382, Carbohydrates 8g, Cholesterol 166mg, Total Fat 22g, Protein 38g, Sodium 220mg, Calcium 50mg

Green Beans with Southern Catfish

Prep Time: 15 minutes, Cook Time: 10 minutes, Serves: 2

Ingredients:

- 2 catfish fillets
- ¾ oz. green beans, trimmed
- 1 large egg, beaten lightly
- 2 tablespoons of mayonnaise
- 1 teaspoon light brown sugar
- 1/3 cup breadcrumbs
- ½ teaspoon of apple cider vinegar

Instructions:

1. Keep the green beans in a bowl. Apply cooking spray liberally.
2. Sprinkle some brown sugar, a pint of salt, and crushed red pepper (optional).
3. Keep in your air fryer basket. Cook at 400 degrees F until it becomes tender and brown.
4. Transfer to your bowl. Use aluminum foil to cover.
5. Toss the catfish in flour. Shake off the excesses.
6. Dip the pieces into the egg. Coat all sides evenly. Sprinkle breadcrumbs.
7. Keep fish in the fryer basket. Apply cooking spray.
8. Now cook at 400 degrees F until it is cooked thoroughly and brown.
9. Sprinkle pepper and ¼ teaspoon of salt.
10. Whisk together the vinegar, sugar, and mayonnaise in a bowl.
11. Serve the fish with tartar sauce and green beans.

Nutrition Facts Per Serving

Calories 562, Carbohydrates 31g, Total Fat 34g, Protein 33g, Fiber 7g, Sugar 16g, Sodium 677mg

Fish Sticks

Prep Time: 10 minutes, Cook Time: 10 minutes, Serves: 4

Ingredients:

- 16 oz. fillets of tilapia or cod
- 1 egg
- ¼ cup all-purpose flour
- ¼ cup Parmesan cheese, grated
- 1 teaspoon of paprika
- ½ cup bread crumbs

Instructions:

1. Preheat your air fryer to 200 degrees C or 400 degrees F.
2. Use paper towels to pat dry your fish.
3. Cut into 1 x 3-inch sticks.
4. Keep flour in a dish. Beat the egg in another dish.
5. Bring together the paprika, cheese, bread crumbs and some pepper in another shallow dish.
6. Coat the sticks of fish in flour.
7. Now dip them in the egg and coat the bread crumbs mix.
8. Apply cooking spray on the air fryer basket.
9. Keep the sticks in your basket. They shouldn't touch.
10. Apply cooking spray on each fish stick.
11. Cook in the air fryer for 3 minutes. Flip over and cook for another 2 minutes.

Nutrition Facts Per Serving

Calories 217, Carbohydrates 17g, Cholesterol 92mg, Total Fat 5g, Protein 26g, Fiber 0.7g, Sugar 0g, Sodium 245mg

Grilled Fish Fillet in Pesto Sauce

Prep Time: 10 minutes, Cook Time: 8 minutes, Serves: 2

Ingredients:
- 2 fish fillets, white fish
- 1 tablespoon of olive oil
- 2 cloves of garlic
- 1 bunch basil
- 1 tablespoon Parmesan cheese, grated

Instructions:
1. Heat your air fryer to 180 degrees C.
2. Brush oil on your fish fillets. Season with salt and pepper.
3. Keep in your basket and into the fryer.
4. Cook for 6 minutes.
5. Keep the basil leaves with the cheese, olive oil, and garlic in your food processor.
6. Pulse until it becomes a sauce. Include salt to taste.
7. Keep fillets on your serving plate. Serve with pesto sauce.

Nutrition Facts Per Serving

Calories 1453, Carbohydrates 3g, Cholesterol 58mg, Total Fat 141g, Protein 43g, Fiber 1g, Sugar 0g, Sodium 1773mg

Air Fryer Salmon

Prep Time: 6 minutes, Cook Time: 6 minutes, Serves: 2

Ingredients:

- 5 oz. filets of salmon
- ¼ cup mayonnaise
- ¼ cup of pistachios, chopped finely
- 1-1/2 tablespoons of minced dill
- 2 tablespoons of lemon juice

Instructions:

1. Preheat your air fryer to 400 degrees F.
2. Spray olive oil on the basket.
3. Season your salmon with pepper to taste. You can also apply the all-purpose seasoning.
4. Combine the mayonnaise, lemon juice, and dill in a bowl.
5. Pour a spoonful on the fillets.
6. Top the fillets with chopped pistachios. Be generous.
7. Spray olive oil on the salmon lightly.
8. Air fry your fillets now for 5 minutes.
9. Take out the salmon carefully with a spatula from your air fryer.
10. Keep on a plate. Garnish with dill.

Nutrition Facts Per Serving

Calories 305, Carbohydrates 1g, Cholesterol 43mg, Total Fat 21g, Protein 28g, Fiber 2g, Sugar 3g, Sodium 92mg

Lemon Dill Mahi Mahi

Prep Time: 5 minutes, Cook Time: 15 minutes, Serves: 2

Ingredients:

- 2 fillets of Mahi Mahi, thawed
- 2 lemon slices
- 1 tablespoon olive oil
- 1 tablespoon lemon juice
- 1 tablespoon dill, chopped

Instructions:

1. Combine the olive oil and lemon juice in a bowl. Stir.
2. Keep the fish fillets on a parchment paper sheet.
3. Brush the lemon juice mix on each side. Coat heavily.
4. Season with pepper and salt.
5. Add the chopped dill on top.
6. Keep the fillets of Mahi Mahi in your air fryer basket.
7. Cook at 400° F for 12 minutes.
8. Take out. Serve immediately.

Nutrition Facts Per Serving

Calories 95, Carbohydrates 2g, Cholesterol 21mg, Total Fat 7g, Protein 6g, Sugar 0.2g, Sodium 319mg

Tartar Sauce Fish Sticks

Prep Time: 15 minutes, Cook Time: 15 minutes, Serves: 4

Ingredients:

- 1 oz. fillets of cod, cut into small sticks
- ¾ cup mayonnaise
- 1-1/2 cups bread crumbs
- 2 tablespoons of dill pickle relish
- 1 teaspoon seafood seasoning

Instructions:

1. Combine the relish, seafood seasoning, and the mayonnaise in a bowl.
2. Include the fish. Stir gently to coat.
3. Preheat your air fryer to 200 degrees C or 400 degrees F.
4. Keep the bread crumbs on your plate.
5. Coat the sticks of fish in the crumbs one at a time.
6. Transfer the fish sticks to your air fryer basket. Place in one single layer. They shouldn't be touching each other.
7. Cook for 10 minutes.
8. Take out from the basket. Set aside for a minute.
9. Keep in a plate lined with a paper towel before serving.

Nutrition Facts Per Serving

Calories 491, Carbohydrates 30g, Cholesterol 16mg, Total Fat 39g, Protein 5g, Sugar 1g, Fiber 0.2g, Sodium 634mg

Lobster Tails with Garlic Butter-Lemon

Prep Time: 10 minutes, Cook Time: 10 minutes, Serves: 2

Ingredients:

- 2 lobster tails
- 1 teaspoon lemon zest
- 4 tablespoons of butter
- 1 garlic clove, grated
- 2 wedges of lemon

Instructions:

1. Butterfly the lobster tails. Use kitchen shears to cut by length through the top shell's center and the meat.
2. Cut to the bottom portion of the shells.
3. Now spread halves of the tail apart.
4. Keep these tails in the basket of your air fry. The lobster meat should face up.
5. Melt the butter in your saucepan.
6. Add the garlic and lemon zest. Heat for 30 seconds.
7. Transfer two tablespoons of this mix to a bowl.
8. Brush on your lobster tails. Remove the remaining brushed butter.
9. Season with pepper and salt.
10. Cook in your air fryer at 195 degrees C or 380 degrees F. The lobster meat should turn opaque in about 5 or 7 minutes.
11. Apply the reserved butter over the lobster meat.
12. You can serve with lemon wedges.

Nutrition Facts Per Serving

Calories 462, Carbohydrates 3g, Cholesterol 129mg, Total Fat 42g, Protein 18g, Sugar 0g, Fiber 1g, Sodium 590mg

Blackened Fish Tacos

Prep Time: 15 minutes, Cook Time: 15 minutes, Serves: 4

Ingredients:

- 1 oz. fillets of tilapia
- 1 can black beans, rinsed and drained
- 1 tablespoon olive oil
- 2 corn ears, cut the kernels
- 4 corn tortillas
- ¼ cup blackened seasoning

Instructions:

1. Preheat your oven to 200 degrees C or 400 degrees F.
2. Bring together the corn, black beans, olive oil and salt in your bowl.
3. Stir gently until the corn and beans are coated evenly. Set aside.
4. Keep the fillets of fish on a work surface. Use paper towels to pat dry.
5. Apply cooking spray on each fillet lightly.
6. Sprinkle half of the blackened seasoning on the top.
7. Now flip over the fillets. Apply the cooking spray. Sprinkle the seasoning.
8. Keep the fish in your air fryer basket, in one single layer.
9. Cook for 2-3 minutes. Flip over and cook for another 2 minutes.
10. Take out and place on a plate.
11. Keep the corn and bean mix in the air fryer basket.
12. Cook for 8 minutes. Stir after 4 minutes.
13. Keep your fish in the corn tortillas. Apply the corn and bean mix on top.

Nutrition Facts Per Serving

Calories 376, Carbohydrates 43g, Cholesterol 42mg, Total Fat 8g, Protein 33g, Sugar 2g, Fiber 11g, Sodium 2210mg

Beef, Lamb, and Pork

Italian-Style Meatballs

Prep Time: 10 minutes, **Cook Time**: 35 minutes, **Serves**: 12

Ingredients:
- 10 oz. lean beef, ground
- 3 garlic cloves, minced
- 5 oz. turkey sausage
- 2 tablespoons shallot, minced
- 1 large egg, lightly beaten
- 2 tablespoons of olive oil
- 1 tablespoon of rosemary and thyme, chopped

Instructions:
1. Preheat your air fryer to 400 degrees F.
2. Heat oil and add the shallot. Cook for 1-2 minutes.
3. Add the garlic now and cook. Take out from the heat.
4. Add the garlic and cooked shallot along with the egg, turkey sausage, beef, rosemary, thyme, and salt. Combine well by stirring.
5. Shape the mixture gently into 1-1/2 inch small balls.
6. Keep the balls in your air fryer basket.
7. Cook your meatballs at 400 degrees F. They should turn light brown.
8. Take out. Keep warm.
9. Serve the meatballs over rice or pasta.

Nutrition Facts Per Serving

Calories 175, Carbohydrates 0g, Total Fat 15g, Fiber 0g, Protein 10g, Sugar 0g, Sodium 254mg

Ranch Pork Chops

Prep Time: 5 minutes, Cook Time: 15 minutes, Serves: 4

Ingredients:

- 4 pork chops, boneless and center-cut
- 2 teaspoons salad dressing mix

Instructions:

1. Keep your pork chops on a plate.
2. Apply cooking spray on both sides lightly.
3. Sprinkle the seasoning mixture on both sides.
4. Allow to sit at room temperature for 5 minutes.
5. Apply cooking spray on the basket.
6. Preheat your air fryer to 200 degrees C or 390 degrees F.
7. Keep the chops in the air fryer. It shouldn't get overcrowded.
8. Cook for 5 minutes. Now flip your chops and cook for another 5 minutes.
9. Allow it to rest before serving.

Nutrition Facts Per Serving

Calories 276, Carbohydrates 1g, Cholesterol 107mg, Total Fat 12g, Fiber 0g, Protein 41g, Sugar 0g, Sodium 148mg

BBQ Baby Ribs

Prep Time: 5 minutes, Cook Time: 35 minutes, Serves: 4

Ingredients:
- 3 lb. ribs of baby back pork
- 1 tablespoon each of white and brown sugar
- 1 teaspoon smoked paprika
- 1 teaspoon of garlic, granulated
- 1/3 cup barbeque sauce

Instructions:
1. Preheat your air fryer to 175 degrees C or 350 degrees F.
2. Strip off the membrane from the rib's back. Cut into 4 equal size portions.
3. Bring together the brown and white sugar, paprika, pepper, granulated garlic, and the green seasoning (optional) in a bowl.
4. Rub the spice mix all over your pork ribs.
5. Keep in the fryer basket.
6. Now cook the ribs for 25 minutes. Turn once after 12 minutes.
7. Brush the BBQ sauce.
8. Air fry this for another 5 minutes.

Nutrition Facts Per Serving

Calories 752, Carbohydrates 16g, Cholesterol 176mg, Total Fat 60g, Fiber 0.7g, Protein 37g, Sugar 12g, Sodium 415mg

Air-Fried Meatloaf

Prep Time: 10 minutes, Cook Time: 45 minutes, Serves: 4

Ingredients:

- 8 oz. pork, ground
- 8 oz. veal, ground
- 1 large egg
- ¼ cup bread crumbs
- 1.4 cup cilantro, chopped
- 1 teaspoon of olive oil
- 2 teaspoons chipotle chili sauce

Instructions:

1. Preheat your air fryer to 200 degrees C or 400 degrees F.
2. Bring together the veal and pork in a baking dish. Make sure that it goes into your air fryer basket.
3. Create a well. Now add the cilantro, egg, bread crumbs, salt, and pepper.
4. Use your hands to mix well and create a loaf.
5. Combine the olive oil and chipotle chili sauce in a bowl. Whisk well.
6. Keep it aside.
7. Cook the meatloaf in your air fryer. Take it out and add the juicy mix.
8. Bring back the meatloaf to the fryer. Bake for 7 minutes.
9. Turn the fryer off. Allow the meatloaf to rest for 6 minutes inside.
10. Take it out and let it rest for 5 more minutes.
11. Slice before serving.

Nutrition Facts Per Serving

Calories 311, Carbohydrates 13g, Cholesterol 123mg, Total Fat 19g, Fiber 0.7g, Protein 22g, Sugar 8g, Sodium 536mg

Pork Skewers with Mango Salsa & Black Bean

Prep Time: 30 minutes, Cook Time: 10 minutes, Serves: 4

Ingredients:

- 1 lb. pork tenderloin, cut into small cubes
- ½ can black beans, rinsed and drained
- 1 mango, peeled, seeded, and chopped
- 4-1/2 teaspoons of onion powder
- 4-1/2 teaspoons thyme, crushed
- 1 tablespoon vegetable oil
- ¼ teaspoon cloves, ground

Instructions:

1. Stir in the thyme, onion powder, salt, and cloves in a bowl to create the seasoning mixture.
2. Keep a tablespoon of this for the pork. Transfer the remaining to an airtight container for later.
3. Preheat your air fryer to 175 degrees C or 350 degrees F.
4. Thread the chunks of pork into the skewers.
5. Brush oil on the pork. Sprinkle the seasoning mix on all sides.
6. Keep in your air fryer basket.
7. Cook for 5 minutes.
8. Mash one-third of the mango in your bowl in the meantime.
9. Stir the remaining mango in, and also salt, pepper, and black beans.
10. Serve the salsa with the pork skewers.

Nutrition Facts Per Serving

Calories 372, Carbohydrates 35g, Cholesterol 49mg, Total Fat 16g, Fiber 7g, Protein 22g, Sugar 18g, Sodium 1268mg

Rosemary Garlic Lamb Chops

Prep Time: 3 minutes, Cook Time: 12 minutes, Serves: 2

Ingredients:

- 4 chops of lamb
- 1 teaspoon olive oil
- 2 teaspoon garlic puree
- Fresh garlic
- Fresh rosemary

Instructions:

1. Keep your lamb chops in the fryer grill pan.
2. Season the chops with pepper and salt. Brush some olive oil.
3. Add some garlic puree on each chop.
4. Cover the grill pan gaps with garlic cloves and rosemary sprigs.
5. Refrigerate the grill pan to marinate.
6. Take out after 1 hour. Keep in the fryer and cook for 5 minutes.
7. Use your spatula to turn the chops over.
8. Add some olive oil and cook for another 5 minutes.
9. Set aside for a minute.
10. Take out the rosemary and garlic before serving.

Nutrition Facts Per Serving

Calories 678, Carbohydrates 1g, Cholesterol 257mg, Total Fat 38g, Protein 83g, Sugar 0g, Sodium 200mg

Lamb Sirloin Steak

Prep Time: 40 minutes, Cook Time: 15 minutes, Serves: 4

Ingredients:
- 1 oz. lamb sirloin steaks, boneless
- 5 garlic cloves
- 1 teaspoon fennel, ground
- ½ onion
- 1 teaspoon cinnamon, ground

Instructions:
1. Add all the ingredients in your blender bowl other than the lamb chops.
2. Pulse and blend until you see the onion minced fine. All the ingredients should be blended well.
3. Now keep your lamb chops in a big-sized bowl.
4. Slash the meat and fat with a knife.
5. The marinade should penetrate.
6. Include the spice paste. Mix well.
7. Refrigerate the mixture for half an hour.
8. Keep the steaks of lamb in your air fryer basket.
9. Cook, flipping once.

Nutrition Facts Per Serving

Calories 189, Carbohydrates 3g, Total Fat 9g, Protein 24g, Fiber 1g

Braised Lamb Shanks

Prep Time: 15 minutes, Cook Time: 2 hours, 30 minutes, Serves: 4

Ingredients:

- 4 lamb shanks
- 4 crushed garlic cloves
- 2 tablespoons of olive oil
- 3 cups of beef broth
- 2 tablespoons balsamic vinegar

Instructions:

1. Rub pepper and salt on your lamb shanks. Keep in the baking pan.
2. Rub the smashed garlic on the lamb well.
3. Now cut the shanks with olive oil.
4. Keep underneath your lamb.
5. Keep the pan into the rack.
6. Roast for 20 minutes at 425 degrees F. Change to low for 2 hours at 250 F.
7. Add vinegar and 2 cups of broth.
8. Including the remaining broth after the 1st hour.

Nutrition Facts Per Serving

Calories 453, Carbohydrates 6g, Cholesterol 121mg, Total Fat 37g, Protein 24g, Fiber 2g, Sodium 578mg

Sweet Potato, Brown Rice, and Lamb

Prep Time: 15 minutes, Cook Time: 10 minutes, Serves: 2

Ingredients:

- ¼ cup lamb, cooked and puréed
- ½ cup cooked brown rice
- ¼ cup of sweet potato purée

Instructions:

1. Keep all the ingredients in your bowl.
2. Pulse until you achieve the desired consistency.
3. Process with milk to get a smoother consistency.
4. Store in an airtight container. Refrigerate.

Nutrition Facts Per Serving

Calories 37, Carbohydrates 5g, Cholesterol 7mg, Total Fat 1g, Protein 2g, Fiber 1g, Sodium 6mg

Roast Beef

Prep Time: 5 minutes, Cook Time: 45 minutes, Serves: 6

Ingredients:
- 2 oz. beef roast
- 1 tablespoon olive oil
- 2 teaspoon thyme and rosemary
- 1 teaspoon of salt
- 1 onion, medium

Instructions:
1. Preheat your air fryer to 200 degrees C or 390 degrees F.
2. Mix the rosemary, oil, and salt on a plate.
3. Use paper towels to pat dry your beef roast.
4. Keep it on a plate. Coat the oil-herb mix on the outside.
5. Keep your beef roast in the air fryer basket.
6. Peel the onion. Cut it in half. Keep the halves next to your roast.
7. Cook for 12 minutes.
8. Change the temperature to 180 degrees C or 360 degrees F.
9. Cook for another 25 minutes.
10. Take it out and cover using kitchen foil.
11. Let it rest for 5 minutes.
12. Carve it thinly against the grain.
13. Serve with steamed or roasted vegetables, gravy, and wholegrain mustard.

Nutrition Facts Per Serving

Calories 221, Carbohydrates 2g, Cholesterol 83mg, Total Fat 9g, Protein 33g, Fiber 1g, Sugar 1g, Sodium 282mg

Beef Kabobs

Prep Time: 30 minutes, Cook Time: 10 minutes, Serves: 4

Ingredients:

- 1 oz. beef ribs, cut into small 1-inch pieces
- 2 tablespoons soy sauce
- 1/3 cup low-fat sour cream
- 1 bell pepper
- ½ onion

Instructions:

1. Mix soy sauce and sour cream in a bowl.
2. Keep the chunks of beef in the bowl. Marinate for 30 minutes' minimum.
3. Now cut the onion and bell pepper into one-inch pieces.
4. Soak 8 skewers in water.
5. Thread the bell pepper, onions, and beef on the skewers. Add some pepper.
6. Cook for 10 minutes in your pre-heated air fryer. Turn after 5 minutes.

Nutrition Facts Per Serving

Calories 297, Carbohydrates 4g, Cholesterol 84mg, Total Fat 21g, Protein 23g, Sugar 2g, Sodium 609mg, Calcium 49mg

Mushrooms with Steak

Prep Time: 5 minutes, Cook Time: 10 minutes, Serves: 4

Ingredients:

- 1 oz. sirloin beef steak, cut into small 1-inch cubes
- ¼ cup Worcestershire sauce
- 8 oz. sliced button mushrooms
- 1 tablespoon of olive oil
- 1 teaspoon chili flakes, crushed

Instructions:

1. Combine the mushrooms, steak, olive oil Worcestershire sauce, and chili flakes in your bowl.
2. Keep it refrigerated for 4 hours minimum.
3. Take out 30 minutes before cooking.
4. Preheat your oven to 200 degrees C or 400 degrees F.
5. Drain out the marinade from your steak mixture.
6. Now keep the mushrooms and steak in the air fryer basket.
7. Cook for 5 minutes in the air fryer.
8. Toss and then cook for another 5 minutes.
9. Transfer the mushrooms and steak to a serving plate.

Nutrition Facts Per Serving

Calories 261, Carbohydrates 6g, Cholesterol 60mg, Total Fat 17g, Protein 21g, Sugar 3g, Fiber 0.9g, Sodium 213mg

Poultry

Asian Deviled Eggs

Prep Time: 15 minutes, Cook Time: 15 minutes, Serves: 12

Ingredients:
- 6 eggs
- 2 tablespoons of mayonnaise
- 1 teaspoon soy sauce, low-sodium
- 1-1/2 teaspoons of sesame oil
- 1 teaspoon Dijon mustard

Instructions:
1. Keep the eggs on the air fryer rack. Make sure that there is adequate space between them.
2. Set the temperature to 125 degrees C or 160 degrees F.
3. Air fry for 15 minutes.
4. Take out the eggs from your air fryer. Keep in an ice water bowl for 10 minutes.
5. Take them out of the water. Now peel and cut them in half.
6. Scoop out the yolks carefully. Keep in a food processor.
7. Add the sesame oil, mayonnaise, Dijon mustard, and soy sauce.
8. Process until everything combines well. The mixture should be creamy.
9. Fill up your piping bag with this yolk mixture. Distribute evenly into the egg whites. They should be heaping full.
10. You can garnish with green onions and sesame seeds (optional).

Nutrition Facts Per Serving

Calories 70, Carbohydrates 1g, Cholesterol 94mg, Total Fat 6g, Protein 3g, Sugar 0g, Fiber 0.1g, Sodium 102mg

Peruvian Chicken Drumsticks & Green Crema

Prep Time: 15 minutes, Cook Time: 15 minutes, Serves: 6

Ingredients:

- 6 chicken drumsticks
- 2 garlic cloves, grated
- 1 tablespoon of olive oil
- 1 tablespoon honey
- 1 cup of baby spinach leaves, with stems removed
- ¼ cup cilantro leaves
- ¾ cup of sour cream

Instructions:

1. Bring together the honey, garlic, pepper, and salt in a bowl.
2. Add the drumsticks. Coat well by tossing.
3. Keep the drumsticks in a vertical position in the basket. Keep them leaning against the wall of the basket.
4. Cook in your air fryer at 200 degrees C or 400 degrees F for 15 minutes.
5. In the meantime, combine the sour cream, cilantro leaves, pepper and salt in a food processor bowl.
6. Process until the crema has become smooth.
7. Drizzle the crema sauce over your drumsticks.

Nutrition Facts Per Serving

Calories 337, Carbohydrates 6g, Cholesterol 82mg, Total Fat 25g, Protein 22g, Sugar 3g, Fiber 0.5g, Sodium 574mg

Popcorn Chicken

Prep Time: 15 minutes, Cook Time: 10 minutes, Serves: 4

Ingredients:
- 1 oz. chicken breast halves, boneless and skinless
- ½ teaspoon paprika
- ¼ teaspoon mustard, ground
- ¼ teaspoon of garlic powder
- 3 tablespoons of cornstarch

Instructions:
1. Cut the chicken into small pieces and keep in a bowl.
2. Combine the paprika, garlic powder, mustard, salt, and pepper in another bowl.
3. Reserve a teaspoon of your seasoning mixture. Sprinkle the other portion on the chicken. Coat evenly by tossing.
4. Combine the reserved seasoning and cornstarch in a plastic bag.
5. Combine well by shaking.
6. Keep your chicken pieces in the bag. Seal it and shake for coating evenly.
7. Now transfer the chicken to a mesh strainer. Shake the excess cornstarch.
8. Keep aside for 5-10 minutes. The cornstarch should start to get absorbed into your chicken.
9. Preheat your air fryer to 200 degrees C or 390 degrees F.
10. Apply some oil on the air fryer basket.
11. Keep the chicken pieces inside. They should not overlap.
12. Apply cooking spray.
13. Cook until the chicken isn't pink anymore.

Nutrition Facts Per Serving

Calories 156, Carbohydrates 6g, Cholesterol 65mg, Total Fat 4g, Protein 24g, Sugar 0g, Fiber 0.3g, Sodium 493mg

Blackened Chicken Breast

Prep Time: 10 minutes, Cook Time: 20 minutes, Serves: 2

Ingredients:

- 2 chicken breast halves, skinless and boneless
- 1 teaspoon thyme, ground
- 2 teaspoons of paprika
- 2 teaspoons vegetable oil
- ½ teaspoon onion powder

Instructions:

1. Combine the thyme, paprika, onion powder, and salt together in your bowl.
2. Transfer the spice mix to a flat plate.
3. Rub vegetable oil on the chicken breast. Coat fully.
4. Roll the chicken pieces in the spice mixture. Press down, ensuring that all sides have the spice mix.
5. Keep aside for 5 minutes.
6. In the meantime, preheat your air fryer to 175 degrees C or 360 degrees F.
7. Keep the chicken in the air fryer basket. Cook for 8 minutes.
8. Flip once and cook for another 7 minutes.
9. Transfer the breasts to a serving plate. Serve after 5 minutes.

Nutrition Facts Per Serving

Calories 427, Carbohydrates 3g, Cholesterol 198mg, Total Fat 11g, Protein 79g, Sugar 1g, Fiber 2g, Sodium 516mg

Air Fryer Chicken Wings

Prep Time: 10 minutes, Cook Time: 30 minutes, Serves: 4

Ingredients:
- 1-1/2 oz. chicken wings
- 1 teaspoon garlic powder
- 1 teaspoon kosher salt
- 1 tablespoon of butter, unsalted and melted
- ½ cup hot sauce

Instructions:
1. Keep your chicken wings in 1 layer. Use paper towels to pat them dry.
2. Sprinkle garlic powder and salt evenly.
3. Now keep these wings in your air fryer at 380°F.
4. Cook for 20 minutes. Toss after every 5 minutes. The wings should be cooked through and tender.
5. Bring up the temperature to 400 degrees F.
6. Cook for 5-8 minutes until it has turned golden brown and crispy.
7. Toss your wings with melted butter (optional) before serving.

Nutrition Facts Per Serving

Calories 291, Carbohydrates 1g, Total Fat 23g, Protein 20g, Sugar 0.3g, Fiber 0g, Sodium 593mg

Nashville Chicken

Prep Time: 20 minutes, Cook Time: 20 minutes, Serves: 8

Ingredients:

- 2 oz. chicken breast, boneless
- 2 tablespoons hot sauce
- ½ cup of olive oil
- 3 large eggs
- 3 cups all-purpose flour
- 1 teaspoon of chili powder
- 1-1/2 cups buttermilk

Instructions:

1. Toss together the chicken, hot sauce, salt, and pepper in a bowl. Combine well.
2. Cover and refrigerate for three hours.
3. Pour flour into your bowl.
4. Now whisk the buttermilk and eggs together. Add 1 tablespoon of hot sauce.
5. For dredging your chicken, keep it in the flour first. Toss evenly for coating.
6. Keep it in your buttermilk mix. Then into the flour.
7. Keep them on your baking sheet.
8. Set the air fryer at 380 degrees. Place the tenders in your fryer.
9. Cook for 10 minutes.
10. For the sauce, whisk the spices and olive oil. Combine well.
11. Pour over the fried chicken immediately.

Nutrition Facts Per Serving

Calories 668, Carbohydrates 44g, Cholesterol 156mg, Total Fat 40g, Protein 33g, Sugar 5g, Fiber 2g, Sodium 847mg

Turkish Chicken Kebab

Prep Time: 45 minutes, Cook Time: 15 minutes, Serves: 4

Ingredients:

- 1 oz. Chicken thighs, boneless and skinless
- ¼ cup Greek yogurt, plain
- 1 tablespoon tomato paste
- 1 tablespoon vegetable oil
- ½ teaspoon cinnamon, ground

Instructions:

1. Stir together the tomato paste, Greek yogurt, oil, cinnamon, salt, and pepper in a bowl. The spices should blend well into the yogurt.
2. Cut the chicken into 4 pieces.
3. Now include your chicken pieces into the mixture. Make sure that the chicken is coated well with the mixture.
4. Refrigerate for 30 minutes' minimum.
5. Take out chicken from your marinade.
6. Keep in your air fryer basket in a single layer.
7. Set your fryer to 370 degrees F. Cook the chicken pieces for 8 minutes.
8. Flip over and cook for another 4 minutes.

Nutrition Facts Per Serving

Calories 375, Carbohydrates 4g, Cholesterol 112mg, Total Fat 31g, Protein 20g, Sugar 1g, Fiber 1g

Hard-Boiled Eggs

Prep Time: 16 minutes, Cook Time: 16 minutes, Serves: 6

Ingredients:

- 6 eggs, large

Instructions:

1. Keep the eggs on your air fryer's wire rack.
2. Set the temperature to 250.
3. Take out the eggs once they are done.
4. Place them in a bowl with ice water.
5. Peel them off and serve.

Nutrition Facts Per Serving

Calories 91, Carbohydrates 1g, Total Fat 7g, Protein 6g, Sugar 0g, Fiber 0g, Sodium 62mg

Egg Frittata

Prep Time: 10 minutes, Cook Time: 15 minutes, Serves: 2

Ingredients:

- 4 eggs
- ¼ cup baby mushrooms, chopped
- ½ cup of milk
- 2 onions, chopped
- ¼ cup cheddar cheese

Instructions:

1. Grease your pan with butter and keep it aside.
2. Whisk together the milk and eggs in a bowl. Blend well.
3. Stir in the mushrooms, onion, cheddar cheese, salt, and pepper. You can also include some hot sauce.
4. Now pour in the egg mix into your pan.
5. Transfer to your air fryer. Cook for 12 minutes at 360 degrees F.

Nutrition Facts Per Serving

Calories 281, Carbohydrates 6g, Cholesterol 348mg, Total Fat 21g, Protein 17g, Sugar 4g, Calcium 229mg, Sodium 826mg

Turkey Breasts

Prep Time: 10 minutes, Cook Time: 40 minutes, Serves: 6

Ingredients:

- 2-3/4 oz. turkey breasts, with skin
- 1 tablespoon rosemary, chopped
- 1 teaspoon chive, chopped
- 2 tablespoons of butter, unsalted
- 1 teaspoon garlic, minced

Instructions:

1. Preheat your air fryer to 175 degrees C or 350 degrees F.
2. Keep the chives, rosemary, garlic, pepper, and salt on your cutting board.
3. Make thin slices of butter and place on the seasonings and herbs. Blend well.
4. Pat the herbed butter on both sides of the turkey breasts.
5. Keep the turkey in the air fryer basket, skin-down side.
6. Fry for 17 minutes.
7. Turn the skin-side up and keep frying for 8 more minutes at 74 degrees C or 165 degrees F.
8. Transfer to a plate. Set aside for 10 minutes.
9. Slice before serving.

Nutrition Facts Per Serving

Calories 287, Carbohydrates 0.3g, Cholesterol 86mg, Total Fat 14g, Protein 40g, Sugar 0g, Fiber 0.1g, Sodium 913mg

Air Fryer Egg Rolls

Prep Time: 30 minutes, Cook Time: 15 minutes, Serves: 16

Ingredients:
- 1 pack of egg roll wrappers
- 2 cups corn, thawed
- 1 can spinach, drained
- 1 can black beans, drained and rinsed
- 1 cup cheddar cheese, shredded

Instructions:
1. Mix the corn, spinach, beans, Cheddar cheese, salt, and pepper in a bowl. This is for the filling.
2. Keep an egg roll wrapper.
3. Moisten lightly all the edges with your finger.
4. Keep a fourth of the filling at the wrapper's center.
5. Now fold a corner over the filling. Tuck the sides in to create a roll.
6. Repeat this process with the other wrappers.
7. Apply cooking spray on the egg rolls.
8. Preheat your air fryer at 199 degrees C or 390 degrees F.
9. Keep your egg rolls in its basket. They should not touch each other.
10. Fry for 7 minutes. Flip and cook for another 4 minutes.

Nutrition Facts Per Serving

Calories 260, Carbohydrates 27g, Cholesterol 25mg, Total Fat 12g, Protein 11g, Sugar 1g, Fiber 4g, Sodium 628mg

Olive-Brined Turkey Breast

Prep Time: 5 minutes, Cook Time: 20 minutes, Serves: 14

Ingredients:

- 3-1/2 oz. turkey breasts, boneless and skinless
- ½ cup buttermilk
- ¾ cup olive brine
- 2 sprigs of thyme
- 1 rosemary sprig

Instructions:

1. Bring together the buttermilk and olive brine.
2. Keep the turkey breast in a plastic bag. Pour the buttermilk-brine mix into this.
3. Add the thyme sprigs and rosemary.
4. Seal and bag. Keep it refrigerated.
5. Take it out after 8 hours. Set it aside and wait for it to reach room temperature.
6. Preheat your air fryer to 175 degrees C or 350 degrees F.
7. Cook the turkey breast for 12 minutes.
8. Flip over and cook for another 5 minutes. The turkey's center shouldn't be pink.

Nutrition Facts Per Serving

Calories 133, Carbohydrates 1g, Cholesterol 82mg, Total Fat 1g, Protein 30g, Sugar 0g, Fiber 0.6g, Sodium 62mg

Bang-Bang Chicken

Prep Time: 10 minutes, Cook Time: 15 minutes, Serves: 6

Ingredients:
- 1 oz. chicken breast tenderloins, small pieces
- ½ cup sweet chili sauce
- 1 cup of mayonnaise
- 1-1/2 cups bread crumbs
- 1/3 cup flour

Instructions:
1. Whisk the sweet chili sauce and mayonnaise together in a bowl.
2. Spoon out 3 quarters of a cup from this. Set aside.
3. Keep flour in a plastic bag. Add the chicken and close this bag. Coat well by shaking.
4. Place the coated chicken in a large bowl with the mayonnaise mix.
5. Combine well by stirring.
6. Keep your bread crumbs in another plastic bag.
7. Place chicken pieces into the bread crumbs. Coat well.
8. Preheat your air fryer to 200 degrees C or 400 degrees F.
9. Transfer the chicken into the basket of your air fryer. Do not overcrowd.
10. Cook for 7 minutes.
11. Flip over and cook for another 4 minutes.
12. Transfer the chicken to a bowl. Pour over the reserved sauce.
13. You can also sprinkle some green onions before serving.

Nutrition Facts Per Serving

Calories 566, Carbohydrates 35g, Cholesterol 60mg, Total Fat 38g, Protein 21g, Sugar 7g, Fiber 1g, Sodium 818mg

Vegetarian and Vegan

Air-Fried Italian-Style Ratatouille

Prep Time: 25 minutes, Cook Time: 25 minutes, Serves: 4

Ingredients:

- ½ eggplant, cubed into small pieces
- 1 medium-sized tomato, cubed
- 1 zucchini, cubed
- 2 oregano sprigs, stemmed and chopped
- 1 tablespoon olive oil
- 1 tablespoon of white wine

Instructions:

1. Preheat your air fryer to 200 degrees C or 400 degrees F.
2. Place the zucchini, eggplant, and tomato in a bowl.
3. Now add the oregano, pepper, and salt.
4. Distribute well by mixing.
5. Drizzle in the white wine and oil. Coat the vegetables well.
6. Pour the vegetable mix into your baking dish.
7. Insert this into your air fryer basket.
8. Cook for 15 minutes, stirring once.
9. Stir once more and keep cooking until it gets tender.
10. Turn the air fryer off.
11. Let it rest for 5-7 minutes before serving.

Nutrition Facts Per Serving

Calories 93, Carbohydrates 10g, Cholesterol 0mg, Total Fat 5g, Protein 2g, Sugar 5g, Fiber 3g, Sodium 48mg

Stuffed Pumpkin

Prep Time: 25 minutes, Cook Time: 30 minutes, Serves: 2

Ingredients:
- ½ pumpkin, small
- 1 sweet potato, diced
- 1 parsnip, diced
- 1 carrot, diced
- 1 egg

Instructions:
1. Scrape out the seeds from the pumpkin.
2. Combine the sweet potato, parsnip, carrot, and the egg in a bowl.
3. Fill up your pumpkin with this vegetable mixture.
4. Preheat your air fryer to 175 degrees C or 350 degrees F.
5. Keep your stuffed pumpkin in the fryer's basket.
6. Cook for 25 minutes. It should become tender.

Nutrition Facts Per Serving

Calories 268, Carbohydrates 49g, Cholesterol 93mg, Total Fat 4g, Protein 9g, Sugar 13g, Fiber 10g, Sodium 210mg

Potato-Skin Wedges

Prep Time: 20 minutes, Cook Time: 30 minutes, Serves: 4

Ingredients:
- 4 medium potatoes
- 3 tablespoons of canola oil
- 1 cup of water
- ¼ teaspoon black pepper, ground
- 1 teaspoon paprika

Instructions:
1. Keep the potatoes in a big-sized pot. Add salted water and keep covered. Boil.
2. Bring down the heat to medium. Let it simmer. It should become tender.
3. Drain the water on.
4. Keep in a bowl and place in the refrigerator until it becomes cool.
5. Bring together the paprika, oil, salt, and black pepper in a bowl.
6. Now cut the potatoes into small quarters. Toss them into your mixture.
7. Preheat your air fryer to 200 degrees C or 400 degrees F.
8. Add half of the wedges of potato into the fryer basket. Keep them skin-down. Don't overcrowd.
9. Cook for 15 minutes. It should become golden brown.

Nutrition Facts Per Serving

Calories 276, Carbohydrates 38g, Cholesterol 0mg, Total Fat 12g, Protein 4g, Sugar 2g, Fiber 5g, Sodium 160mg

Air Fryer Pumpkin Keto Pancakes

Prep Time: 5 minutes, Cook Time: 5 minutes, Serves: 2

Ingredients:
- ½ cup pumpkin puree
- 1 teaspoon of vanilla extract
- 2 eggs
- ½ cup peanut butter
- ½ teaspoon baking soda

Instructions:
1. Use parchment paper to line the basket of your air fryer.
2. Apply some cooking spray.
3. Bring together the eggs, peanut butter, pumpkin puree, baking soda, salt, and eggs in a bowl. Combine well by stirring.
4. Place 3 tablespoons of the batter in each pancake. There should be a half-inch space between them.
5. Keep the basket in your air fryer oven.
6. Cook for 4 minutes at 150 degrees C or 300 degrees F.

Nutrition Facts Per Serving

Calories 586, Carbohydrates 20g, Cholesterol 186mg, Total Fat 46g, Protein 23g, Sugar 9g, Fiber 6g, Sodium 906mg

Fried Green Tomatoes

Prep Time: 15 minutes, Cook Time: 20 minutes, Serves: 6

Ingredients:
- 2 tomatoes, cut into small slices
- ½ cup buttermilk
- 2 eggs, beaten lightly
- 1 cup bread crumbs
- 1/3 cup of all-purpose flour
- 1 cup yellow cornmeal

Instructions:
1. Season the slices of tomato with pepper and salt.
2. Take 2 breeding dishes. Keep flour in the first, stir in eggs and buttermilk in the second, and mix cornmeal and bread crumbs in the third.
3. Dredge the slices of tomato in your flour. Shake off any excess.
4. Now dip the tomatoes in the egg mix.
5. Then dip into the bread crumb mix. Coat both sides.
6. Preheat your air fryer to 200 degrees C or 400 degrees F.
7. Brush olive oil on the fryer basket.
8. Keep the slices of tomato in your fryer basket. They shouldn't touch.
9. Brush some olive oil on the tomato tops.
10. Cook for 10 minutes. Flip your tomatoes, brush olive oil and cook for another 5 minutes.
11. Take the tomatoes out. Keep in a rack lined with a paper towel.

Nutrition Facts Per Serving
Calories 246, Carbohydrates 40g, Cholesterol 63mg, Total Fat 6g, Protein 8g, Sugar 3g, Fiber 2g, Sodium 166mg

Roasted Vegetables

Prep Time: 10 minutes, Cook Time: 20 minutes, Serves: 4

Ingredients:

- 1 yellow squash, cut into small pieces
- 1 red bell pepper, seeded and cut into small pieces
- ¼ oz. mushrooms, cleaned and halved
- 1 tablespoon of extra-virgin olive oil
- 1 zucchini, cut into small pieces

Instructions:

1. Preheat your air fryer. Keep the squash, red bell pepper, and mushrooms in a bowl.
2. Add the black pepper, salt, and olive oil. Combine well by tossing.
3. Keep the vegetables in your fryer basket.
4. Air fry them for 15 minutes. They should get roasted. Stir about halfway into the roasting time.

Nutrition Facts Per Serving

Calories 89, Carbohydrates 8g, Cholesterol 0mg, Total Fat 5g, Protein 3g, Sugar 4g, Fiber 2.3g, Sodium 48mg

Baked Potatoes

Prep Time: 5 minutes, Cook Time: 1 hour, Serves: 2

Ingredients:

- 1 tablespoon peanut oil
- 2 large potatoes, scrubbed
- ½ teaspoon of coarse sea salt

Instructions:

1. Preheat your air fryer to 200 degrees C or 400 degrees F.
2. Brush peanut oil on your potatoes.
3. Sprinkle some salt.
4. Keep them in the basket of your air fryer.
5. Cook the potatoes for an hour.

Nutrition Facts Per Serving

Calories 360, Carbohydrates 64g, Cholesterol 0mg, Total Fat 8g, Protein 8g, Sugar 3g, Fiber 8g, Sodium 462mg

Spicy Green Beans

Prep Time: 10 minutes, Cook Time: 25 minutes, Serves: 4

Ingredients:
- ¾ oz. green beans, trimmed
- 1 teaspoon of soy sauce
- 1 tablespoon sesame oil
- 1 garlic clove, minced
- 1 teaspoon of rice wine vinegar

Instructions:
1. Preheat your air fryer to 200 degrees C or 400 degrees F.
2. Keep the green beans in a bowl.
3. Whisk together the soy sauce, sesame oil, garlic, and rice wine vinegar in another bowl.
4. Pour the green beans into it.
5. Coat well by tossing. Leave it for 5 minutes to marinate.
6. Transfer half of the beans to your air fryer basket.
7. Cook for 12 minutes. Shake the basket after 6 minutes.
8. Repeat with the other portion of green beans.

Nutrition Facts Per Serving

Calories 81, Carbohydrates 7g, Cholesterol 0mg, Total Fat 5g, Protein 2g, Sugar 1g, Fiber 3g, Sodium 80mg

Roasted Cauliflower and Broccoli

Prep Time: 10 minutes, Cook Time: 15 minutes, Serves: 6

Ingredients:

- 3 cups cauliflower florets
- 3 cups of broccoli florets
- ¼ teaspoon of sea salt
- ½ teaspoon of garlic powder
- 2 tablespoons olive oil

Instructions:

1. Preheat your air fryer to 200 degrees C or 400 degrees F.
2. Keep your florets of broccoli in a microwave-safe bowl.
3. Cook in your microwave for 3 minutes on high temperature. Drain off the accumulated liquid.
4. Now add the olive oil, cauliflower, sea salt, and garlic powder to the broccoli in the bowl.
5. Combine well by mixing.
6. Pour this mix now into your air fryer basket.
7. Cook for 10 minutes. Toss the vegetables after 5 minutes for even browning.

Nutrition Facts Per Serving

Calories 77, Carbohydrates 6g, Cholesterol 0mg, Total Fat 5g, Protein 2g, Sugar 2g, Fiber 3g, Sodium 103mg

Roasted Okra

Prep Time: 5 minutes, Cook Time: 15 minutes, Serves: 1

Ingredients:
- ½ oz. okra, trimmed ends and sliced pods
- ¼ teaspoon salt
- 1 teaspoon olive oil
- 1/8 teaspoon black pepper, ground

Instructions:
1. Preheat your air fryer to 175 degrees C or 350 degrees F.
2. Bring together the olive oil, okra, pepper, and salt in a mid-sized bowl.
3. Stir gently.
4. Keep in your air fryer basket. It should be in one single layer.
5. Cook for 5 minutes in the fryer. Toss once and cook for another 5 minutes.
6. Toss once more. Cook again for 2 minutes.

Nutrition Facts Per Serving

Calories 138, Carbohydrates 16g, Cholesterol 0mg, Total Fat 6g, Protein 5g, Sugar 3g, Fiber 7g, Sodium 600mg

Sweet Potato Hash

Prep Time: 10 minutes, Cook Time: 15 minutes, Serves: 6

Ingredients:

- 2 sweet potatoes, cubed into small pieces
- 2 tablespoons of olive oil
- 1 teaspoon black pepper, ground
- 1 tablespoon of smoked paprika
- 1 teaspoon dill weed, dried

Instructions:

1. Preheat your air fryer to 200 degrees C or 400 degrees F.
2. Toss the olive oil, sweet potatoes, paprika, pepper, and salt in a bowl.
3. Keep this mixture in your air fryer.
4. Now cook for 12 minutes.
5. Check first, and then stir after 8 minutes. Stir after another 2 minutes. It should turn brown and crispy.

Nutrition Facts Per Serving

Calories 203, Carbohydrates 31g, Cholesterol 3mg, Total Fat 7g, Protein 4g, Sugar 6g, Fiber 5g, Sodium 447mg

Fried Chickpeas

Prep Time: 5 minutes, Cook Time: 20 minutes, Serves: 4

Ingredients:
- 1 can chickpeas, rinsed and drained
- 1 tablespoon olive oil
- 1 tablespoon of nutritional yeast
- 1 teaspoon garlic, granulated
- 1 teaspoon of smoked paprika

Instructions:
1. Spread the chickpeas on paper towels. Cover using a second paper towel later.
2. Allow them to dry for half an hour.
3. Preheat your air fryer to 180 degrees C or 355 degrees F.
4. Bring together the nutritional yeast, chickpeas, smoked paprika, olive oil, salt, and garlic in a mid-sized bowl. Coat well by tossing.
5. Now add your chickpeas to the fryer.
6. Cook for 16 minutes until they turn crispy. Shake them in 4-minute intervals.

Nutrition Facts Per Serving

Calories 133, Carbohydrates 17g, Cholesterol 0mg, Total Fat 5g, Protein 5g, Sugar 0g, Fiber 4g, Sodium 501mg

Corn Nuts

Prep Time: 10 minutes, Cook Time: 25 minutes, Serves: 8

Ingredients:
- 1 oz. white corn
- 1-1/2 teaspoons salt
- 3 tablespoons of vegetable oil

Instructions:
1. Keep the corn in a bowl. Cover this with water. Keep aside for 8 hours minimum for hydration.
2. Drain the corn. Spread it on a baking sheet. They should be in an even layer.
3. Use paper towels to pat dry. Also air dry for 15 minutes.
4. Preheat your air fryer to 200 degrees C or 400 degrees F.
5. Transfer the corn to a bowl. Add salt and oil. Stir to coat evenly.
6. Keep the corn in your air fryer basket in an even layer.
7. Cook for 8 minutes.
8. Shake the basket and cook for 8 minutes more.
9. Shake the basket once more. Cook for 5 more minutes.
10. Transfer to a plate lined with a paper towel.
11. Set aside for allowing the corn nuts to cool. They should be crisp.

Nutrition Facts Per Serving

Calories 240, Carbohydrates 36g, Cholesterol 0mg, Total Fat 8g, Protein 6g, Sugar 1g, Fiber 7g, Sodium 438mg

Potato Tots

Prep Time: 15 minutes, Cook Time: 35 minutes, Serves: 24

Ingredients:
- 2 peeled sweet potatoes
- Olive oil cooking spray
- ½ teaspoon Cajun seasoning
- Sea salt to taste

Instructions:
1. Boil a pot of water. Add the sweet potatoes in it.
2. Keep boiling until you can pierce them using a fork.
3. It should take about 15 minutes. Don't over boil, as they can get too messy for grating. Drain off the liquid. Allow it to cool.
4. Grate the potatoes in a bowl.
5. Now mix your Cajun seasoning carefully.
6. Create tot-shaped cylinders with this mixture.
7. Spray some olive oil on your fryer basket.
8. Keep the tots in it. They should be in 1 row and shouldn't be touching each other or the basket's sides.
9. Apply some olive oil spray on the tots.
10. Heat your air fryer to 200 degrees C or 400 degrees F.
11. Cook for 8 minutes.
12. Flip over and cook for 8 more minutes after applying the olive oil spray again.

Nutrition Facts Per Serving

Calories 22, Carbohydrates 5g, Cholesterol 0mg, Total Fat 0g, Protein 0.4g, Sugar 1g, Fiber 0.7g, Sodium 36mg

Desserts

Air Fryer Beignets

Prep Time: 10 minutes, Cook Time: 15 minutes, Serves: 7

Ingredients:
- ½ cup all-purpose flour
- 1 egg, separated
- ½ teaspoon of baking powder
- 1-1/2 teaspoons melted butter
- ¼ cup white sugar
- ½ teaspoon of vanilla extract

Instructions:
1. Preheat your air fryer to 185 degrees C or 370 degrees F.
2. Whisk together the sugar, flour, butter, egg yolk, vanilla extract, baking powder, salt, and water in a bowl. Combine well by stirring.
3. Use an electric hand mixer to beat the white portion of the egg in a bowl.
4. Fold this into the batter.
5. Now use a small ice cream scoop to add the mold.
6. Keep the mold into the air fryer basket.
7. Fry for 10 minutes in your air fryer.
8. Take out the mold and the pop beignets carefully.
9. Flip them over on a round of parchment paper.
10. Now transfer the parchment round with the beignets into the fryer basket.
11. Cook for 4 more minutes.

Nutrition Facts Per Serving

Calories 99, Carbohydrates 16g, Cholesterol 29mg, Total Fat 3g, Protein 2g, Sugar 9g, Fiber 0.2g, Sodium 74mg

Sugar and Cinnamon Doughnuts

Prep Time: 25 minutes, Cook Time: 16 minutes, Serves: 9

Ingredients:

- 2 egg yolks
- 1-1/2 teaspoons baking powder
- 2-1/4 cups of all-purpose flour
- 2 tablespoons of butter
- ½ cup of white sugar
- ½ cup sour cream

Instructions:

1. Press butter and ½ cup of white sugar together in a bowl. It should get crumbly.
2. Add the egg yolks. Stir to combine well.
3. Now sift baking powder, flour, and salt into another bowl.
4. Place a third of the flour mix and half sour cream into your egg-sugar mix.
5. Combine well by stirring.
6. Mix the remaining sour cream and flour in.
7. Refrigerate this dough until you can use it.
8. Now mix 1/3rd cup of sugar.
9. Roll your dough to half-inch thickness on a work surface.
10. Cut the dough into 9 circles. Create a small circle at the center of each circle. The shape should be like a doughnut.
11. Preheat your air fryer to 175 degrees C or 350 degrees F.
12. Brush half of the melted butter on both sides of your doughnut.
13. Transfer half of the doughnuts into your air fryer basket.
14. Cook for 6 minutes. Apply melted butter on the doughnuts.

Nutrition Facts Per Serving

Calories 336, Carbohydrates 44g, Cholesterol 66mg, Total Fat 16g, Protein 4g, Sugar 19g, Fiber 1g, Sodium 390mg

Apple Fritters

Prep Time: 15 minutes, Cook Time: 10 minutes, Serves: 4

Ingredients:

- 1 apple – cored, peeled, and chopped
- 1 cup all-purpose flour
- 1 egg
- ½ cup milk
- 1-1/2 teaspoons of baking powder
- 2 tablespoons white sugar

Instructions:

1. Preheat your air fryer to 175 degrees C or 350 degrees F.
2. Keep parchment paper at the bottom of your fryer.
3. Apply cooking spray.
4. Mix together ¼ cup sugar, flour, baking powder, egg, milk, and salt in a bowl.
5. Combine well by stirring.
6. Sprinkle 2 tablespoons of sugar on the apples. Coat well.
7. Combine the apples into your flour mixture.
8. Use a cookie scoop and drop the fritters with it to the air fryer basket's bottom.
9. Now air fry for 5 minutes.
10. Flip the fritters once and fry for another 3 minutes. They should be golden.

Nutrition Facts Per Serving

Calories 307, Carbohydrates 65g, Cholesterol 48mg, Total Fat 3g, Protein 5g, Sugar 39g, Fiber 2g, Sodium 248mg

Air-Fried Butter Cake

Prep Time: 10 minutes, Cook Time: 15 minutes, Serves: 4

Ingredients:

- 1 egg
- 7 tablespoons of butter, room temperature
- 1-2/3 cups all-purpose flour
- ½ cup white sugar
- 6 tablespoons of milk

Instructions:

1. Preheat your air fryer to 180 degrees C or 350 degrees F.
2. Apply cooking spray on a small tube pan.
3. Beat ¼ cup and 2 tablespoons of butter. It should be creamy and light.
4. Include the egg. Mix until it gets fluffy and smooth.
5. Stir in the salt and flour now.
6. Add milk. Mix the batter thoroughly.
7. Transfer the batter to your pan. Level the surface with a spoon's back.
8. Keep this pan in the basket of your air fryer.
9. Bake until you see a toothpick coming out clean when inserted.
10. Take out the cake. Set aside for cooling for 5 minutes.

Nutrition Facts Per Serving

Calories 596, Carbohydrates 60g, Cholesterol 102mg, Total Fat 36g, Protein 8g, Sugar 20g, Fiber 1.4g, Sodium 210mg

Apple Pies

Prep Time: 30 minutes, Cook Time: 15 minutes, Serves: 4

Ingredients:

- 2 medium apples, diced
- 6 tablespoons brown sugar
- 1 teaspoon of cornstarch
- 4 tablespoons butter
- ½ tablespoon of grapeseed oil
- 1 teaspoon milk

Instructions:

1. Combine butter, apples, and brown sugar in your non-stick skillet.
2. Cook on medium heat for 5 minutes. The apples should get soft.
3. Now dissolve the cornstarch in some cold water.
4. Stir the apple mixture in. Cook until you see the sauce thickening.
5. Take out the apple pie filling. Keep aside for cooling.
6. Unroll your pie crust on a floured surface. Roll out a bit to make the dough surface smooth.
7. Cut your dough into small rectangles. 2 of them should fit into the air fryer.
8. Repeat the process until there are 8 rectangles that are equal.
9. Use water to wet the outer edges of your 4 rectangles.
10. Keep the apple filling at the center. It should be half an inch away from the edges.
11. Roll out your other rectangles. They should be a bit bigger than the ones you have filled up.
12. Keep these rectangles at the top of your filling.
13. Use a fork to crimp the edges for sealing.
14. Now create four small slits at the top portion of your pies.
15. Apply some cooking spray in the air fryer basket.
16. Brush grapeseed oil on the top portion of 2 pies. Keep them in the fryer basket.
17. Bake for 6 minutes. They should become golden brown.
18. Take them out. Repeat with the other 2 pies.
19. Drizzle some milk on the warm pies. Let them dry before serving.

Nutrition Facts Per Serving

Calories 612, Carbohydrates 60g, Cholesterol 31mg, Total Fat 40g, Protein 3g, Sugar 36g, Fiber 3g, Sodium 328mg

Air Fryer Oreos

Prep Time: 5 minutes, Cook Time: 10 minutes, Serves: 9

Ingredients:

- ½ cup pancake mix
- 9 chocolate sandwich cookies like Oreo®
- 1/3 cup water
- 1 tablespoon of confectioners' sugar

Instructions:

1. Mix water and the pancake mix. Combine well.
2. Use parchment paper to line the basket of your air fryer.
3. Apply some cooking spray.
4. Now dip the cookies into your pancake mix. Keep in the fryer basket.
5. They should not touch each other.
6. Preheat your air fryer to 200 degrees C or 400 degrees F.
7. Cook for 4 minutes.
8. Flip over. Cook for 3 more minutes until they turn golden brown.
9. Sprinkle some confectioners' sugar.

Nutrition Facts Per Serving

Calories 78, Carbohydrates 14g, Cholesterol 0mg, Total Fat 2g, Protein 1g, Sugar 5g, Fiber 0.3g, Sodium 156mg

Roasted Bananas

Prep Time: 2 minutes, Cook Time: 7 minutes, Serves: 1

Ingredients:

- 1 banana, sliced into diagonal pieces
- Avocado oil cooking spray

Instructions:

1. Take parchment paper and line the air fryer basket with it.
2. Preheat your air fryer to 190 degrees C or 375 degrees F.
3. Keep your slices of banana in the basket. They should not touch.
4. Apply avocado oil to mist the slices of banana.
5. Cook for 5 minutes.
6. Take out the basket. Flip the slices carefully.
7. Cook for 2 more minutes. The slices of banana should be caramelized and browning. Take them out from the basket.

Nutrition Facts Per Serving

Calories 121, Carbohydrates 27g, Cholesterol 0mg, Total Fat 1g, Protein 1g, Sugar 14g, Fiber 3g, Sodium 1mg

Banana Cake

Prep Time: 10 minutes, Cook Time: 30 minutes, Serves: 4

Ingredients:
- 1 mashed banana
- 1 egg
- 1/3 cup brown sugar
- 3-1/2 tablespoons of butter, room temperature
- 1 cup flour
- 2 tablespoons of honey

Instructions:
1. Preheat your air fryer to 160 degrees C or 320 degrees F.
2. Apply cooking spray on a small tube pan.
3. Beat the butter and sugar together in your bowl. It should turn creamy.
4. Bring together the egg, banana, and honey in another bowl.
5. Now whisk this banana mix into your butter mixture. It should be smooth.
6. Stir in the salt and flour into this mixture.
7. Mix the batter until it gets smooth.
8. Keep in the pan and transfer to the air fryer basket.
9. Bake until you see a toothpick coming out clean from the cake.

Nutrition Facts Per Serving

Calories 419, Carbohydrates 57g, Cholesterol 73mg, Total Fat 19g, Protein 5g, Sugar 30g, Fiber 2g, Sodium 531mg

Gluten-Free Cherry Crumble

Prep Time: 15 minutes, Cook Time: 25 minutes, Serves: 4

Ingredients:

- 3 cups pitted cherries
- 2 teaspoons of lemon juice
- 1/3 cup butter
- 1 cup gluten-free all-purpose baking flour
- 1 teaspoon vanilla powder
- 10 tablespoons of white sugar

Instructions:

1. Cube the butter and refrigerate for about 15 minutes. It should get firm.
2. Preheat your air fryer to 165 degrees C or 325 degrees F.
3. Bring together the pitted cherries, lemon juice, and 2 tablespoons of sugar in your bowl. Mix well.
4. Pour the cherry mix into a baking dish.
5. Now mix 6 tablespoons of sugar and flour in a bowl.
6. Use your fingers to cut in the butter. Particles should be pea-size.
7. Keep them over the cherries. Press down lightly.
8. Stir in the vanilla powder and 2 tablespoons of sugar in your bowl.
9. Dust the sugar topping over flour and cherries.
10. Transfer to your air fryer and bake.
11. Leave it inside for 10 minutes once the baking is done.
12. Set aside for 5 minutes to cool.

Nutrition Facts Per Serving

Calories 576, Carbohydrates 76g, Cholesterol 41mg, Total Fat 28g, Protein 5g, Sugar 49g, Fiber 6g, Sodium 109mg

Easy Apple Pies

Prep Time: 15 minutes, Cook Time: 15 minutes, Serves: 10

Ingredients:

- 2 pie crusts
- 1 can apple pie filling
- 2 tablespoons of cinnamon sugar
- 1 egg, beaten

Instructions:

1. Keep 1 pie crust on a floured surface.
2. Roll the dough out with your rolling pin.
3. Take a cookie-cutter. Now create 10 circles by cutting your pie crust.
4. Do this with the 2nd pie crust as well. You should have 20 circles.
5. Fill up half of each circle with the apple pie filling.
6. Keep the second circle on top, creating a mini pie. Make sure not to overfill.
7. Press down edges of your mini peas. Seal.
8. Brush beaten egg on the tops. Sprinkle some cinnamon sugar.
9. Preheat your air fryer to 175 degrees C or 360 degrees F.
10. Apply cooking spray on the fryer basket lightly.
11. Keep your mini peas in the basket. There should be space for air circulation.
12. Bake for 7 minutes. They should turn golden brown.

Nutrition Facts Per Serving

Calories 296, Carbohydrates 35g, Cholesterol 16mg, Total Fat 16g, Protein 3g, Sugar 0g, Fiber 2g, Sodium 225mg

Chocolate Cake

Prep Time: 10 minutes, Cook Time: 15 minutes, Serves: 4

Ingredients:

- 3-1/2 tablespoons of butter, softened
- ¼ cup white sugar
- 1 tablespoon of apricot jam
- 1 egg
- 1 tablespoon cocoa powder, unsweetened
- 6 tablespoons of all-purpose flour

Instructions:

1. Preheat your air fryer to 160 degrees C or 320 degrees F.
2. Apply cooking spray on a small tube pan.
3. Use an electric mixer to beat the butter and sugar together in your bowl. It should get creamy and light.
4. Add the jam and egg. Combine well by mixing.
5. Now sift in the cocoa powder, flour, and salt. Make sure to mix well.
6. Pour the batter into your pan. Take a spoon and with its backside, level the batter surface.
7. Transfer pan to your air fryer basket.
8. Cook for 10 minutes. A toothpick should come out clean from the cake's center.

Nutrition Facts Per Serving

Calories 283, Carbohydrates 25g, Cholesterol 73mg, Total Fat 19g, Protein 3g, Sugar 15g, Fiber 2g, Sodium 130mg

Snacks and Appetizers

Coconut Shrimp

Prep Time: 30 minutes, Cook Time: 15 minutes, Serves: 6

Ingredients:

- 1-1/2 teaspoons black pepper, ground
- ½ cup all-purpose flour
- 2 eggs
- 1/3 cup bread crumbs
- 2/3 cup flaked coconut, unsweetened
- ¼ cup lime juice
- ¼ cup of honey

Instructions:

1. Stir together the pepper and flour in a dish.
2. Beat the eggs lightly in another dish.
3. Stir together the bread crumbs and coconut together in a third dish.
4. Hold the shrimp by its tail. Dredge it in the flour mix, shaking off excess.
5. Now dip your floured shrimp in the egg. Drip off any excess.
6. Dredge the coconut mixture in. Press to adhere.
7. Keep on a plate. Apply cooking spray.
8. Preheat your air fryer to 200 degrees C or 400 degrees F.
9. Place half of the shrimp in your fryer. Cook for 3 minutes.
10. Turn once and cook for another 3 minutes. They should turn golden.
11. Apply salt for seasoning.
12. In the meantime, whisk together the lime juice and honey in a bowl. This is for your dip.
13. Finally, sprinkle the dip on your fried shrimp.

Nutrition Facts Per Serving

Calories 312, Carbohydrates 28g, Cholesterol 147mg, Total Fat 16g, Protein 14g, Sugar 13g, Fiber 2g, Sodium 316mg

Crumbed Chicken Tenderloins

Prep Time: 15 minutes, Cook Time: 12 minutes, Serves: 4

Ingredients:

- ½ cup dry bread crumbs
- 1 egg
- 8 chicken tenderloins
- 2 tablespoons of vegetable oil

Instructions:

1. Preheat your air fryer to 175 degrees C or 350 degrees F.
2. Whisk the egg in a bowl.
3. Now mix oil and bread crumbs together in another bowl. This mixture should be crumbly and loose.
4. Dip the chicken tenderloins into the egg bowl. Shake off excesses.
5. Next, dip the chicken into your crumb mix. It should be fully and evenly covered.
6. Keep tenderloins into your air fryer basket.
7. Cook for 10 minutes, until it isn't pink anymore at the center.

Nutrition Facts Per Serving

Calories 270, Carbohydrates 10g, Cholesterol 109mg, Total Fat 14g, Protein 26g, Sugar 1g, Fiber 0.6g, Sodium 171mg

Basic Hot Dogs

Prep Time: 5 minutes, Cook Time: 5 minutes, Serves: 4

Ingredients:
- 4 hot dogs
- 4 hot dog buns

Instructions:
1. Preheat your air fryer to 200 degrees C or 390 degrees F.
2. Keep the buns in your fryer basket. Cook for 2-3 minutes.
3. Transfer them to a plate.
4. Keep your hot dogs in the air fryer basket. Cook for 3 minutes.
5. Place them in the buns.

Nutrition Facts Per Serving

Calories 317, Carbohydrates 23g, Cholesterol 24mg, Total Fat 21g, Protein 9g, Sugar 4g, Fiber 1g, Sodium 719mg

Garlic-Parsley Baby Potatoes

Prep Time: 5 minutes, Cook Time: 20 minutes, Serves: 4

Ingredients:

- 1 oz. baby potatoes, cut into small quarters
- ½ teaspoon garlic, granulated
- 1 tablespoon of avocado oil
- ½ teaspoon parsley, dried
- ¼ teaspoon salt

Instructions:

1. Preheat your air fryer to 175 degrees C or 350 degrees F.
2. Combine the oil and potatoes in your bowl. Coat well by tossing.
3. Include ¼ teaspoon of parsley and ¼ teaspoon of granulated garlic.
4. Repeat the same process for the remaining parsley and garlic.
5. Transfer potatoes to the basket of your air fryer.
6. Cook for 20 minutes, tossing occasionally. It should turn golden brown.

Nutrition Facts Per Serving

Calories 89, Carbohydrates 20g, Cholesterol 0mg, Total Fat 0.1g, Protein 2g, Sugar 1g, Fiber 2.6g, Sodium 153mg

Scotch Eggs

Prep Time: 15 minutes, Cook Time: 15 minutes, Serves: 6

Ingredients:

- 2 eggs, beaten lightly
- 6 hard-boiled and shelled eggs
- 3 tablespoons of Greek yogurt
- 1/8 teaspoon curry powder
- 1 tablespoon mayonnaise
- 1 cup bread crumbs
- 1 oz. pork sausage
- 1/3 cup flour

Instructions:

1. Combine the mayonnaise, yogurt, curry powder, pepper, and salt in a bowl.
2. Keep it refrigerated until you can use it.
3. Platen the 6 pork sausage portions into thin patties.
4. Place an egg at the center of each patty. Wrap sausage around these eggs. Seal all the sides.
5. Preheat your air fryer to 200 degrees C or 390 degrees F.
6. Take flour in a bowl. Beat the eggs into a second bowl.
7. Keep bread crumbs on a plate.
8. Now dip the egg wrapped sausage into flour and then into the beaten egg. Allow the excess portions to drip off.
9. Roll the bread crumbs in. Place on a plate.
10. Apply cooking spray on your fryer basket. Keep the eggs into it. Remember, you shouldn't be overcrowding.
11. Cook for 10 minutes. Turn the eggs after 5 minutes.

Nutrition Facts Per Serving

Calories 501, Carbohydrates 21g, Cholesterol 284mg, Total Fat 37g, Protein 21g, Sugar 3g, Fiber 0.4g, Sodium 945mg

Wrapped Bacon Chicken Thighs

Prep Time: 10 minutes, Cook Time: 25 minutes, Serves: 4

Ingredients:

- ½ garlic clove, minced
- ½ butter stick, softened
- ¼ teaspoon basil, dried
- 1-1/2 oz. chicken thighs, boneless and skinless
- 1/3 oz. bacon, thick-cut

Instructions:

1. Combine the garlic, softened butter, pepper, salt, and basil in your bowl.
2. Take a wax paper piece and keep the butter on it.
3. Roll it up to create a butter log.
4. Refrigerate it until it becomes firm.
5. Lay a strip of bacon on a wax paper piece.
6. Keep your chicken thighs on the bacon's top. Sprinkle some garlic.
7. Now open your chicken thigh. Keep 1 to 2 teaspoons on cold butter at its middle.
8. Tuck an end of the bacon into the center of the thigh.
9. Fold this over the chicken. Roll your bacon around the thigh.
10. Preheat your air fryer to 190 degrees C or 370 degrees F.
11. Keep the chicken thighs in your air fryer basket.
12. Cook for 20 minutes. The chicken shouldn't be pink anymore. The juices should be running clear.

Nutrition Facts Per Serving

Calories 568, Carbohydrates 1g, Cholesterol 150mg, Total Fat 48g, Protein 33g, Sugar 0g, Fiber 0.2g, Sodium 441mg

Korean Chicken Wings

Prep Time: 10 minutes, Cook Time: 40 minutes, Serves: 4

Ingredients:

- 2 oz. chicken wings
- 3 tablespoons of Korean hot pepper paste
- 1 tablespoon of soy sauce
- 1 teaspoon garlic powder
- 2 teaspoons garlic, minced
- ½ cup cornstarch
- 1 teaspoon ginger root, minced

Instructions:

1. Combine the soy sauce, hot pepper paste (gochujang), ginger, garlic, pepper, and salt in your saucepan.
2. Boil on medium heat. Bring down the heat. Allow 5 minutes for simmering.
3. Preheat your air fryer to 200 degrees C or 400 degrees F.
4. Keep the wings in a bowl. Toss with garlic powder, pepper, and salt.
5. Add the cornstarch. Toss the wings until they are coated completely.
6. Shake the wings and keep them in the basket of your air fryer. See to it that they are not touching.
7. Fry for 10 minutes in your air fryer.
8. Shake the basket and fry for 10 more minutes.
9. Flip the wings and cook for 7 minutes. The juices should run clear.
10. Dip the wings in sauce. You can garnish with sesame seeds and green onions.

Nutrition Facts Per Serving

Calories 370, Carbohydrates 45g, Cholesterol 48mg, Total Fat 14g, Protein 16g, Sugar 24g, Fiber 1g, Sodium 1247mg

Mozzarella Sticks

Prep Time: 20 minutes, Cook Time: 15 minutes, Serves: 4

Ingredients:

- 1/3 cup all-purpose flour
- 1 tablespoon cornmeal
- 1-1/2 teaspoon of garlic powder
- 1 cup bread crumbs
- ¼ teaspoon onion powder
- ½ teaspoon flakes of parsley
- ¼ teaspoon oregano, dried

Instructions:

1. Place flour, cornmeal, water, garlic powder, and salt in a bowl.
2. Mix to create a batter. Get the consistency of pancake batter.
3. Stir in the parsley, onion powder, bread crumbs, salt, and pepper in another shallow and wide bowl.
4. Coat flour on the mozzarella sticks lightly.
5. Dip the sticks in your batter. Toss the bread crumb mix in. Coat well.
6. Now keep the sticks in your baking sheet in one layer.
7. Refrigerate for an hour minimum.
8. Preheat your air fryer to 200 degrees C or 400 degrees F.
9. Keep the mozzarella sticks in your fryer basket. Apply cooking spray lightly.
10. Cook them for 5 minutes. Flip the sticks and cook for another 5 minutes.

Nutrition Facts Per Serving

Calories 307, Carbohydrates 39g, Cholesterol 23mg, Total Fat 11g, Protein 13g, Sugar 1g, Fiber 0.7g, Sodium 936mg

Fried Pickles

Prep Time: 10 minutes, Cook Time: 10 minutes, Serves: 8

Ingredients:

- 2 tablespoons of sriracha sauce
- ½ cup mayonnaise
- 1 egg
- ½ cup all-purpose flour
- 2 tablespoons of milk
- ¼ teaspoon garlic powder
- 1 jar dill pickle chips

Instructions:

1. Mix the sriracha sauce and mayonnaise together in a bowl.
2. Refrigerate until you can use it.
3. Heat your air fryer to 200 degrees C or 400 degrees F.
4. Drain the pickles. Use paper towels to dry them.
5. Now mix the milk and egg together in another bowl.
6. Also mix the cornmeal, flour, garlic powder, pepper, and salt in a third bowl.
7. Dip the pickle chips in your egg mix, and then in the flour mix. Coat both sides lightly. Press the mixture into chips lightly.
8. Apply cooking spray in the fryer basket.
9. Keep the chips in the fryer's basket.
10. Cook for 4 minutes. Flip over and cook for another 4 minutes.
11. Serve with the sriracha mayo.

Nutrition Facts Per Serving

Calories 198, Carbohydrates 15g, Cholesterol 26mg, Total Fat 14g, Protein 3g, Sugar 1g, Fiber 2g, Sodium 1024mg

Air Fryer Lumpia

Prep Time: 15 minutes, Cook Time: 20 minutes, Serves: 16

Ingredients:
- 1 oz. Italian hot sausage links
- ½ cup carrots, chopped
- ½ cup onions, diced and sliced
- ½ cup water chestnut, chopped
- 2 garlic cloves, minced

Instructions:
1. Take out casing from the sausage. Cook on medium heat for 4-5 minutes. It should turn light brown.
2. Add the onions, water chestnut, and carrot.
3. Cook while stirring. The onions should become translucent and soft.
4. Now include the garlic. Cook for 1 more minute. Season with salt.
5. Keep stirring to combine well. Take out from the heat.
6. Keep a spring roll wrapper and at its center, place one-fourth of the filling.
7. Fold the bottom corner. Tuck the sides in, forming a roll.
8. Moisten the edges using water. Apply avocado oil spray.
9. Preheat your air fryer to 198 degrees C or 390 degrees F.
10. Keep the rolls in the fryer basket and cook for 4 minutes.
11. Flip once and cook for 4 more minutes. The skins should get crispy.

Nutrition Facts Per Serving

Calories 111, Carbohydrates 7g, Cholesterol 12mg, Total Fat 7g, Protein 5g, Sugar 1g, Fiber 1g, Sodium 471mg

Printed by BoD"in Norderstedt, Germany